The Mountain Biker's Guide to Ski Resorts

The Mountain Biker's Guide to Ski Resorts

Where to Ride Downhill in New York, New England, and Eastern Canada

Robert M. Immler

Backcountry Publications
Woodstock · Vermont

If you find that any significant changes have occurred on the routes described in this guide, please let the author and publisher know so that corrections may be made in future editions. Other comments and suggestions are also welcome. Address all correspondence to:

Bicycling Editor
Backcountry Publications
PO Box 748
Woodstock, VT 05091

Please be advised that there are hazards inherent to this sport. Although the author has been careful to point out potentially dangerous situations, neither he nor the publisher can take responsibility for any accident or injury that might occur along the routes described in this guide.

Library of Congress Cataloging-in-Publication Data

Immler, Robert.
    The mountain biker's guide to ski resorts : where to ride downhill in New York, New England, and Eastern Canada / Robert M. Immler.
        p.   cm.
    ISBN 0-88150-371-1 (alk. paper)
    1. All terrain cycling—New York (State)—Guidebooks. 2. All terrain cycling—New England—Guidebooks. 3. All terrain cycling—Canada, Eastern—Guidebooks. 4. Ski resorts—New York (State)—Guidebooks. 5. Ski resorts—New England—Guidebooks. 6. Ski resorts—Canada, Eastern—Guidebooks. 7. New York (State)—Guidebooks. 8. New England—Guidebooks. 9. Canada, Eastern—Guidebooks. I. Title.
GV1045.5.N7I44   1998
796.6'3'0974—dc21   97–43218   CIP

Book design by Sally Sherman and Chelsea Dippel
Cover photo by Robert M. Immler
Interior photographs by the author, unless otherwise noted
Maps by XNR Productions, © 1998 Backcountry Publications
Published by Backcountry Publications, a division of
The Countryman Press, PO Box 748, Woodstock, VT 05091
Distributed by W. W. Norton & Company, Inc., 500 Fifth Avenue,
New York, NY 10110
Printed in Canada
10 9 8 7 6 5 4 3 2 1

Dedication

This book is dedicated to the memory of Paul Kluth (1924–1996). He was the leader on my introduction to bicycle touring, a Sierra Club trip to Hawaii that planted a love of the islands, increased my love of bicycling, and inspired me to write my first book, *Bicycling in Hawaii*. We co-led two subsequent trips to Hawaii, rode several times from San Francisco to Los Angeles, and toured the Sierras. In 1976 we both rode across the United States. I'll miss his strength and his sense of humor.

Thanks

I want to thank the following people for their help in researching this book: Ken Bolier, Fred Sperber, Vern Haskins, and Kim Armstrong of Killington; Jon Lamb for giving me a mini tour of Killington; Melissa Gullotti and Kelly Pawlak of Mount Snow; Tammy Steeves of the Appalachian Mountain Club; Leslie Parker, Julie Gilman, and Dennis Welsh of Loon Mountain; Stephanie Young, Conrad Klefos, and Scott Erlandson of Jay Peak; Jim Miller and Pat McNally of Bretton Woods; Chip Laring and Ken Beaulieu of Sunday River; Bruce McCulley of Whiteface; Yves Juneau of Mont-Tremblant; D. J. Hansen of the Sugarloaf Visitor Information Bureau; Elan Plamandon, Steve Colgan, and Guylaine Prive of Bromont; Angela Webster and Mark Lotti of Sugarloaf; Suzanne Roy of Mont-Sainte-Anne; Martin Beland, who introduced me to Bromont via his Internet page; Ed Sawyer of Waterville Valley; Myra Foster of Stratton; Thad Osterhoat and Joe Barclay of Gore Mountain; Roger Haydock for his help with geology; and Marlies Ouwinga and Carisa M. Flood of Cranmore.

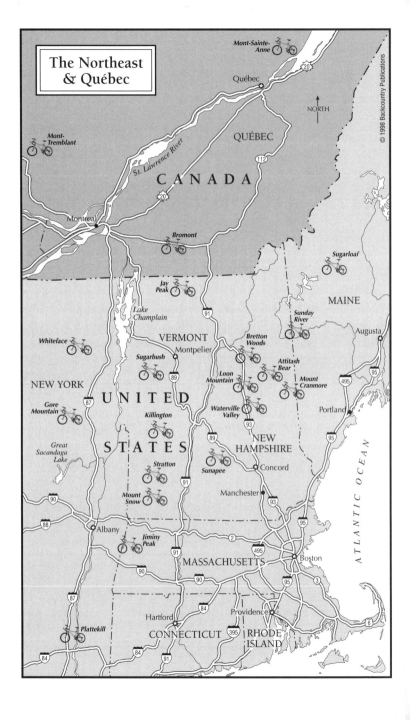

The Northeast & Québec

Mont-Sainte-Anne

Québec

NORTH

CANADA

QUÉBEC

St. Lawrence River

Mont-Tremblant

Montreal

Bromont

Sugarloaf

Jay Peak

Lake Champlain

MAINE

Whiteface

VERMONT

Sunday River

Augusta

Montpelier

Bretton Woods

Attitash Bear

NEW YORK

Sugarbush

Loon Mountain

Mount Cranmore

Gore Mountain

Killington

Waterville Valley

Portland

Great Sacandaga Lake

UNITED

STATES

NEW HAMPSHIRE

Stratton

Sunapee

Concord

ATLANTIC OCEAN

Mount Snow

Manchester

Albany

Jiminy Peak

Boston

MASSACHUSETTS

Hartford

Providence

Plattekill

CONNECTICUT

RHODE ISLAND

Contents

The trails at Loon Mountain, New Hampshire
offer matchless views of the White Mountains.

Introduction

Ponce de Leon sought the fountain of youth; prospectors search for the Lost Dutchman Mine; and cyclists seek the fabled Downhill Loop. Of course the latter will never be found, but in the Northeast, lift-accessed mountain biking comes pretty close.

Bicycling and New England

New England is the birthplace not only of American independence, but also of American cycling. A Boston lawyer, Alfred Chandler, is said to have been the first American cyclist. And in a park in Newport, Rhode Island, there is a plaque that says that the founders of the League of American Wheelmen . . . GATHERED IN NEWPORT ON MAY 30, 1880 FOR THE PROTECTION OF THE RIGHTS, NEEDS AND SAFETY OF BICYCLISTS.

Why did American cycling begin here?

The Atlantic Ocean was the 19th century's version of our information superhighway. Technical advances began in Europe, but New England—closest to Europe—had the manufacturing skill to turn European ideas into American reality.

In 1883 Springfield, Massachusetts, hosted the first bicycling show in the United States. Eighteen companies showed the latest in high-wheelers to a small number of shoppers. Three years later a show was held in Boston at the same time as a meeting of the League of American Wheelmen. Bicycle trade shows soon spread throughout the East and the Midwest. Philadelphia hosted an exhibit in 1891, where the then brand-new safety bicycle was introduced to the American public. The promoters took in $800, a significant amount for the time, and planned more shows. Starting in 1894, large bicycle shows were held each year in Chicago and New York. Robert A. Smith, in his *A Social History of the Bicycle,* points out that ". . . one observer even went so far as to applaud the shows for their democratizing influence because one rubbed elbows with mechanics and laborers, something that never happened at the horse and dog shows."

Cycling was so popular that it became the focus of one of the top 10 song hits of the Gay Nineties, Harry Dacre's "Bicycle Built for Two." Cycling allowed women to wear pants in public for the first time, and cycling clothing, such as pedal pushers, was worn by some people in the general population, even when not on bikes. Today, police officers patrolling on bicycles is a newsworthy event, but Boston officers were patrolling the parks on bicycles during the 1890s.

Skiing

Bicycling wasn't the only sport to cross the Atlantic in the 19th century. Skiing also arrived from Europe. It may have been introduced to America by Sir Arthur Conan Doyle on a trip to Rudyard Kipling's home in Vermont, but it developed at New Hampshire's Dartmouth College. The school's Winter Carnival introduced Americans to ski jumping in 1911 and European-style slalom racing in 1925.

In those days you might spend an hour climbing to the top of a run and then 10 minutes skiing down. There had to be an easier way, though. Then some ingenious person jacked up a Model T and used a tireless wheel and rope to pull skiers to the top of a slope. Thus, the first rope tow was born, and the seeds for a new industry were planted.

Origins of the Mountain Bike

In the summer of 1977, I was living in Southern California and heard rumors of odd bicycles being built in Northern California's

Marin County. It seems people were constructing copies of old Schwinns, but with modern, lightweight European bicycle tubing. To these frames they added aluminum wheels with knobby tires, ultra-low gearing developed for touring, brakes developed for tandem bicycles, and lighter copies of motorcycle handlebars and controls.

The result: a bike that because of interest in cruisers and old cycles looked right. A bike that because of its upright handlebars was more comfortable for those who found the dropped handlebars to be backbreaking. A bike whose tires allowed it to be ridden on dirt. A bike whose brakes allowed it to be ridden downhill for miles with the calipers applied. And a bike whose gearing allowed it to be ridden uphill.

Then in 1982, sensing that a market existed for a bike like this, a California businessman introduced the first mass-produced mountain bike, the $750 Specialized Stumpjumper. It's now on display in the Smithsonian Institution, in Washington, D.C.

Today there are tandem mountain bikes, mountain bikes for children, aluminum mountain bikes, mountain bikes with suspension, bikes with slick tires for riding on pavement, and even mountain bikes with front and rear disk brakes (to control 70+ mph speeds) for downhill racing. And mountain biking is now an Olympic sport.

For me, the mountain bicycle combines the best of the worlds of cycling and hiking. It allows me to see the same beautiful country as the hiker, while its greater efficiency allows me to enjoy about twice as much scenery in the same amount of time.

I'm not the only one who likes mountain bikes. They account for more than 75 percent of the 12 million bicycles sold annually. And by the way, amazingly, most surveys show that about 80 percent of those mountain bikes are never ridden off pavement. It's sort of the mountain bike equivalent of the sport utility vehicle

13

phenomenon: Thousands of city residents purchase off-road vehicles, shod with "rhino" bars, but never leave town.

What's so special about mountain biking? "In just a few minutes from the city," says one cyclist, "you can be out riding with red-tailed hawks, deer, wildflowers, and not see a soul; or if you do, it'll be one of like mind who's up there for the same reasons you are."

Mountain Bikes and Ski Resorts

A Stratton Mountain advertisement to lure mountain bikers to its slopes reads PUT YOURSELF BEHIND BARS!

That's ironic, because the first mountain bikers to ride at ski resorts may have actually ended up in jail. But today mountain bikers and ski resorts have become the perfect example of "If you can't beat 'em, join 'em." In spring, summer, and fall, the cross-country ski trails, old logging roads, ski runs, and access roads of the Northeast's ski resorts make great places to ride. At first these resorts tried to exclude mountain bikers, fearing that the skidding knobby tires could ruin a ski run. But the resorts discovered that most cyclists stayed off the very steep slopes, the ones most susceptible to erosion. And any erosion of the gentler slopes could be halted by occasionally closing runs and keeping bikes off muddy sections or by building wooden boardwalks for them to ride on.

Soon somebody figured out that instead of riding to the top, many cyclists would prefer paying a few bucks to join the visitors already using the lifts in the "off" season. Suddenly, most ski resorts were a perfect match for mountain bicycling. Moreover, many downhill ski resorts also have cross-country ski areas—and these lend themselves to the beginning mountain biker, for whom a 2000-foot descent down a dirt road would be intimidating. For the graduates of the cross-country trails, every resort has dirt access roads and downhill ski trails, ideal places to

14

Cyclists must yield to both hikers and equestrians while on the trail.

mountain bike. For those who want more challenging runs, many resorts now cut trails, especially for mountain bicycling, through the woods.

Conflicts occasionally arise between mountain bikers and two other groups of trail users: equestrians and hikers. How do these groups get along at ski resorts? Most resorts try to keep cyclists and hikers on different trails. But the general rule of thumb is that cyclists yield to hikers and both yield to the occasional equestrian.

Originally, the partnership between cyclists and ski resorts was somewhat crude. I can remember hooking the nose of my saddle over the side of a chairlift to get it to the top. Now there are special racks for bikes; trail maps; hoses to clean off the bikes; pro bike shops, bike-rental programs, and mountain bike schools; and highly publicized and well-attended races. All this enables the mountain bicyclist to discover that summer has transformed ski runs into meadows filled with wildflowers; the groomers of winter are now mowing the grass.

Preparation for Riding at the Resorts

Helmets: Many cyclists who would never think of diving head-first into the ground think nothing of subjecting themselves to the same risk by riding without a helmet. At most resorts, however, there is no choice. They usually require helmets before a lift ticket can be purchased.

Gloves: Bicycle gloves are another safety item. On a mountain bike they can also be used to help absorb road shock, especially if they are padded.

Insects: Except for the real possibility of contracting Lyme disease through a tick bite, the many insects found in New England are more annoying than hazardous. The most irritating are probably the blackflies, but they exist for only a few weeks in late spring. Usually, you can ride faster than the insects. But I still consider insect repellent with DEET an absolute must, because it is needed on slow climbs and during time off the bike. I once forgot to bring it on a long ride. Whenever I stopped, I was attacked by blackflies, so except at one spot, where it is usually windy enough to blow them away, I had to keep moving. The insects turned a normally enjoyable ride into a miserable ordeal.

Although cyclists ride high and avoid riding directly through brush, you should check yourself carefully after a ride for any signs of the tiny deer ticks or their bites. If you notice a circular "bull's-eye" rash, the sign of a bite from an infected tick, you should see a doctor immediately.

Sunscreen: The use of sunscreen is strongly recommended. You can still get a tan, but use sunscreen to prevent excessive aging and possible skin cancer. Even on cloudy days, the ultraviolet rays of the sun can do substantial damage.

Tools: I always carry a pump and a spare tube. I keep a second spare tube, a patch kit, a chain tool, Allen wrenches, a screwdriver, and spare rear-brake and derailleur cables in the car. I generally don't need tire irons to remove a mountain bike tire.

Northeastern weather: There's an old saying that if you don't like the weather in New England . . . wait 10 minutes! This can be especially true of the mountains of the Northeast. So be prepared for sudden changes in weather. Although it may be a pleasant summer day at the bottom of a hill, a few minutes later the lift may take you into much cooler conditions than you were expecting. But this can also be a blessing. In a sticky northeastern heat wave, a ride up the mountain essentially takes you into the air-conditioned zone.

And if you see or hear a thunderstorm approaching, immediately descend or take shelter. The last place you want to be is on top of a mountain on a metal bicycle.

Suspension: Does a suspension-fork or full-suspension bike make the rides in this book more enjoyable? Yes.

Do you need a full-suspension bike to enjoy the rides? No!

I used a rather ancient Specialized Rockhopper with a Girvin flex stem to do most of the trips in this book. My hands never bothered me, even on the rockiest trail.

Brakes: Brakes that are quite adequate on level ground may be incapable of stopping a bike on a steep—or even a moderate—slope. When you squeeze hard on the brake levers, they should not be able to touch the handlebars. Adjust the brakes if needed or replace the pads and check for frayed brake cables. Two thousand feet above a bike shop is not a good place to discover that your brakes are gone.

Tires: The best brakes in the world won't do you any good if your tires are unsuited for the mountains or are worn. Put on the most aggressive off-road tires you can find.

Riding tips: As the trail you're descending steepens, you'll need to transfer your weight over the rear wheel by standing up on the pedals and moving your body more to the rear. Some cyclists assume that since a lift will be taking them to the top, no effort will be required. Then, after a day of lift-accessed mountain biking, they're surprised to find that they have extremely sore lower leg muscles from standing on the pedals all day.

Mountain Bicycling Regulations

The National Off-Road Bicycling Association (NORBA) has put together eight rules of conduct to promote mountain bicycling safety, to educate the cyclist in minimal environmental impact, and to help counter anticycling propaganda.

Off-pavement bicycling can open exciting new horizons for you. In order to maximize the benefit of your adventure and maintain the quality of the experience for those who will follow you, we urge you to adopt this code as your own.

1. *Yield the right-of-way to other nonmotorized recreationists.*
2. *Use caution when overtaking another, and make your presence known well in advance.*
3. *Maintain control of your speed at all times.*
4. *Stay on designated trails only.*
5. *Do not disturb wildlife or livestock.*
6. *Leave no trace; respect public and private property.*
7. *Always wear an approved helmet when riding.*
8. *Support land access organizations.*

Trip Classifications

The trips: The trips were chosen based on my own experiences, on the suggestions of those working at the resorts, and to give a selection of trips from easy to difficult.

© SHARON McNEILL/SUNDAY RIVER

The use of ski lifts in the off-season opens up a whole new world to mountain bikers.

Trip distances: I measured the distances for the trips with a Cat-Eye Mity-2 Cyclometer.

Elevation loss/gain: Elevation losses/gains were calculated with an Avocet Vertech Alpine altimeter. The figures are for total loss or gain, not just the difference between the summit and the base.

The Internet and e-mail: The Internet is a good way to receive more information on mountain biking in the Northeast. Almost every resort in this book now has a page on the Internet. Most of them include prices, trail maps, suggested routes, current trail conditions, and weather reports. And many of the resorts can be contacted via e-mail.

Hostels: Monroe and Isabel Smith, founders of the American Youth Hostels (AYH), began the hostel movement in Northfield,

19

Massachusetts, in 1934. Today AYH offers inexpensive, cycling-friendly accommodations near some of the resorts in this book.

Order of riding: For the beginner, it's usually recommended that you get the feel of off-road riding by starting out on the less steep, non-lift-accessed, cross-country trails. But the more advanced rider will want to start on the lift-accessed trails and then do the cross-country trails in the early evening after the lift has closed for the day.

Glossary

Singletrack: A trail so narrow that one cyclist can't pass another. Although I'm using the term *singletrack* in this book to refer to trails about 24 inches wide, many land management agencies define it as a trail less than 60 inches in width.

Technical: A very difficult section, either uphill or downhill, that is particularly tricky because of steepness, obstacles, poor traction, or all of the above. It requires excellent balance. More experienced riders attempt to ride a technical section without putting a foot down.

Water bar: A channel dug across a trail to lessen erosion from water (and/or to slow down mountain bikes). I like to release my brakes just before the front wheel enters the water bar. Otherwise, the front wheel may catch in the water bar and you'll go over the handlebars. Angles of some allow you to use the water bars as a ramp for jumps.

Mountain bike races

If you have a chance, visit one of the resorts on a race weekend. Some trails may be closed, but you'll see the latest in mountain bikes and accessories (and may pick up some free goodies) at the trade booths, and can usually demo bikes in a much better setting than a bike shop parking lot. You'll be impressed by how quickly the pros can climb in the cross-country races and you'll be amazed by how fast they descend in the downhill events. And join the crowd, which looks like the gallery following golfers, as they follow the competitors in the observed trials events.

You may want to enter a citizens' race. You can usually spectate for free, but many places charge for parking.

A Note

This book shouldn't be thought of as a complete guide to every trail in the Northeast, but only as a sampler. It allows you to taste rides here and there, but in person, you should try the entire menu. Likewise, the maps in this book should be used in conjunction with the trail maps issued by the ski areas.

This book describes resorts that feature mountain biking and trails that were in existence at the time of writing (1995–97). However, by the time this book is published in 1998, trails that I describe here may have closed, and new trails not mentioned here may have opened up. Some resorts in this book may have discontinued mountain biking, while others may now allow it. So use this book as a guide, but to be on the safe side always call ahead before you visit.

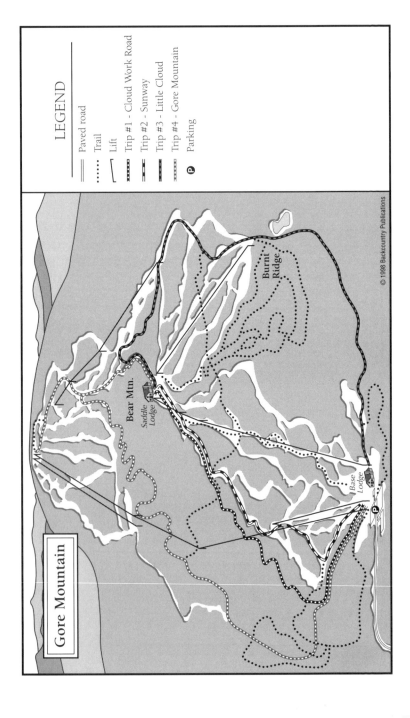

Gore Mountain

LEGEND

Paved road
Trail
Lift
Trip #1 - Cloud Work Road
Trip #2 - Sunway
Trip #3 - Little Cloud
Trip #4 - Gore Mountain
P Parking

Burnt Ridge

Bear Mtn.

Saddle Lodge

Base Lodge

P

© 1998 Backcountry Publications

1
Gore Mountain, New York

Traveling north on I-87 to Gore Mountain, I knew I was in for something special: It's the only resort I know of that advertises mountain biking on billboards.

Gore is a low-key resort that offers a variety of riding to the mountain cyclist. It has the usual access roads, but you can also descend through the meadows of the ski runs and through a maze of technical singletracks. Gore offers only mountain biking and hiking, but if this is not enough, Lake George, 30 minutes southeast, has every attraction and distraction you could desire.

As a young man H.H. Barton worked in a Boston jewelry store. He never forgot the day a man came in and spread a pouch of gem-quality garnets on the counter, and told the story of how he had found them in the Adirondacks. Years later Barton was selling woodworking supplies in the Philadelphia area. He needed a way to produce better sandpaper and remembered the man with the garnets, an excellent source of abrasives. In the 1870s, he went prospecting in the Adirondacks and found the source of the garnets. Not knowing the extent of the vein, he bought the entire mountain. When it turned out that the 300-foot-wide and 3/4-mile-long vein was on just one side of Gore Mountain, the company donated the other side to the state of New York. It also gave the very tip of 3595-foot Gore to the Adirondack Museum, where it is still on display.

How to get there: From the south, take I-87 to exit 23. Take NY 28 west 30 miles to Gore Mountain. From the north, take I-87 to exit 26. Go south on US 9 for 5 miles, then south on NY 8 for 5 miles, to NY 28. Then go 6 miles west to Gore Mountain.

Total miles of biking available: 20+

The lift: A detachable quad takes you up 1500 feet in 11 minutes. Your bike rides on a detachable rack placed on another chair. You ride among pine, ash, birch, and maple trees over a ski run that alternates between exposed rock and fields of wildflowers, including daisies and lupines. The chair lets you out at 3000-foot Bear Mountain, 600 feet below the actual summit of Gore. The Saddle Lodge at Bear Mountain has an emergency phone, rest rooms, and a first-aid station.

Season and hours: July 4 to early September, Friday through Sunday. Early September through mid-October, weekends. 9 AM–4:30 PM.

Prices: Lift tickets are $15, juniors $10; after 12:30 $10, juniors $8. A trail pass costs $7 (juniors $5).

Rental bikes: Full-suspension bikes rent for $35 (half-day $25), front-suspension $25 (half-day $15), junior $20 (half-day $12).

Bike shop: There is a small bike shop in the lodge.

Trail identification: Trails are marked with yellow signs.

Special features: Two-hour guided tours at 10 AM and 1 PM are $35 per person, with family rates available. Gore has three cross-country trails at its base. The lodge offers snacks that you can eat while relaxing in an appropriate Adirondack chair on the lodge's deck. There is a hose to clean the bikes next to the lodge. Emergency phones and picnic tables are located throughout the resort.

Reservation number: 518-251-2411

Internet address: http://www.goremtn.com/gore
E-mail address: info@goremtn.com
Hiking: A single ride on the chairlift is $8, $5 ages 7–12, under 6 free. The Adirondacks abound with hiking trails.
Other activities: Lake George offers accommodations, dining, swimming, and boating. The Great Escape is a modern amusement park. Next door to Gore is the Barton open pit garnet mine. The Adirondack Museum is 20 miles to the northwest at Blue Mountain Lake.
Campground: The Dagget Lake campsite (Glen Athol Road, Warrensburg; 518-623-2198), 12 miles east of Gore, has 60 sites.
Hostel: The St. James Episcopal Church Hall, Montcalm Street (518-668-2634), one block from Lake George, offers hostel facilities.

Suggested itinerary

For the first outing of the day, warm up by taking in the views of the Adirondacks while you descend Gore's easiest run:

Gore Trip 1: Cloud Work Road
Distance: 2.14 miles
Terrain: Work roads
Difficulty: Moderate
Time: 15 minutes
Elevation loss: 1500 feet

0.00 *Leaving the lift, you'll immediately encounter a steep descent. You may want to walk down to the main road, where you turn right. The view of the Adirondacks is spectacular, but you also soon see Loon Lake in the valley below you.*

In the sunlight, the road sparkles as if paved with diamonds.

The inevitable results of a hard day's ride

The "gravel" is the tailings from the nearby Barton garnet mine. On this section of the road, you can spot sections of the rock, mostly black hornblende, with garnet still in it.

0.57 After descending 490 feet in 5 minutes, you pass the junction with the Wolf Peak run. In another 5 minutes, pass the junction with the Doe Brook run.

1.66 After descending 1390 feet in 11 minutes, you go left at the T.

2.14 After descending 1500 feet in 13 minutes, cross a meadow and you're back at the lift.

Now for a trip that descends the same gravel road for a short distance, then goes down the steep Sunway ski run:

Gore Trip 2: Sunway

Distance: *2.01 miles*
Terrain: *Gravel road and ski run*
Difficulty: *Moderate to difficult*
Time: *22 minutes*
Elevation loss: *1500 feet*

0.00 Leave the top of the lift and descend to the right on the gravel road.

0.37 Leave the road and go left onto Sunway.

This is a ski run, so it's easy on skis or a board but very challenging on a mountain bike, as you roll down through the meadow and cross the exposed granite. At the bottom of the run, you go left onto the work road and ride through the meadow in front of the lodge.

2.01 After 22 minutes, you're back at the lift.

After a slight climb, you'll descend on some gravel roads that offer views of the Adirondacks to the north, then encounter some narrow trails and some technical singletracks, on:

Gore Trip 3: Little Cloud

Distance: *4.52 miles*
Terrain: *Ski-area work roads, ski trails, singletracks*
Difficulty: *Moderate to mildly technical*
Time: *45 minutes*
Elevation loss: *1500 feet*
Elevation gain: *200 feet*

0.00 *After getting off the lift, go left and climb the gravel work road.*

0.35 *After gaining 70 feet in 3 minutes, go right onto Little Cloud.*

Through the opening in the trees created by a ski run, you get a great view of the Adirondacks to the north, including Gore's sister resort, Whiteface. The prominent, exposed white rock gives that peak its name.

0.77 *You leave the road and go right onto a trail that goes through the woods.*

1.22 *After descending 500 feet in 13 minutes, Little Cloud #10 climbs steeply to the right, then turns left into the trees again.*

This becomes a fairly technical singletrack as it ascends, descends, and turns through the forest.

1.55 *You leave the singletrack, emerge from the woods, veer left onto a ski run, and descend steeply.*

1.82 *After 22 minutes, go left onto a gravel work road.*

A sign warns skiers and riders that this way is off-limits, but here "riders" refers to snowboarders in winter, not mountain bikers in summer. Soon you pass a snowmaking pond that has picnic tables.

2.81 *The road passes a bridge, but keep straight and don't cross it. You now encounter a fairly steep climb back to the base area.*

4.52 *After 45 minutes, you're back at the lift.*

Now you're ready to ride to the summit of Gore Mountain and then descend via a tough singletrack:

Gore Trip 4: Gore Mountain

Distance: *4.84 miles*
Terrain: *Work roads, ski runs, singletracks*
Difficulty: *Difficult*
Time: *1 hour*
Elevation loss: *2100 feet*
Elevation gain: *580 feet*

0.00 After getting off the lift, start climbing the gravel work road. Where Little Cloud turns to the right, go left and begin a tough climb, which for me required a lot of walking.

While walking I noticed that the rock in this section of the road contains many small garnets.

1.20 After a tough 22 minutes, you've climbed 580 feet.

The summit is wooded but there are clearings that allow views in most directions. There are picnic tables and out-houses near the summit. On the actual summit of Gore Mountain is a steel tower. It used to be a fire lookout, but is now a microwave tower. After you're through on the summit, descend on the work road again.

1.97 After 29 minutes you're at the junction of the work road and Harvey's Run #14, where you go right and descend on a ski trail that becomes a singletrack.

This is a very technical section that repeatedly climbs and drops. Toward the bottom, it merges with #12 Wolf Pack, becomes a work road again, and passes through a section where the resort stores so many old army vehicles—which it uses for resort maintenance—that it's almost a museum.

4.84 After 1 hour, you're back at the lodge.

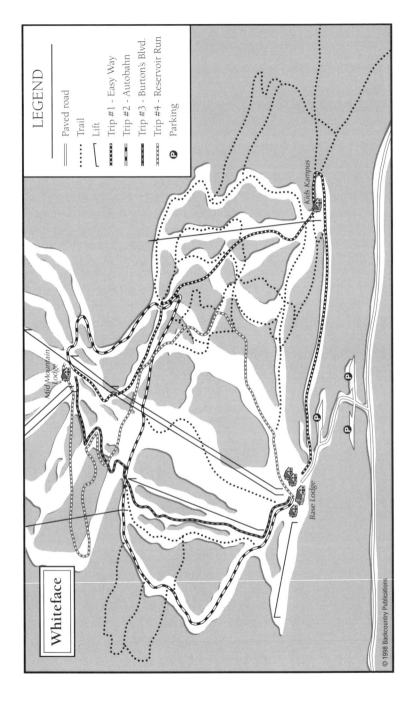

LEGEND

Paved road
Trail
Lift
Trip #1 - Easy Way
Trip #2 - Autobahn
Trip #3 - Burton's Blvd.
Trip #4 - Reservoir Run
P Parking

Whiteface

Mid Mountain Lodge

Base Lodge

Kids Kampus

© 1998 Backcountry Publications

2
Whiteface, New York

Whiteface has a lot to offer the summer visitor: lots of trails for the hiker; commercial attractions related to the Olympics; shopping, restaurants, and bike shops in Lake Placid; and campgrounds with swimming, miniature golf, and games in the evening. The cross-country trails near the bottom offer wonderful cycling, but the downhill trails at Whiteface (at least those accessible by the lower lift) are mostly steep, rocky descents.

When Lake Placid hosted the 1932 and 1980 Winter Olympics, the downhill events were held at nearby Whiteface Mountain. The mountain is now owned by the state of New York and managed by the Olympic Regional Development Committee. The main lodge has a gift shop that carries some cycling accessories, and a snack bar. The Adirondack chairs on the lodge's upper deck make a great place to relax and take in a view of (what else?) the Adirondacks while enjoying a snack.

At the moment, mountain bikers are only allowed to the 2125-foot midmountain. But in the future, you'll be allowed to take the second lift to 3676-foot Little Whiteface, giving Whiteface the greatest vertical drop in the East—almost 2500 feet!

Until then, Whiteface includes fast descents on gravel roads and extensive singletrack and cross-country trails, including trails that go north to the nearby town of Wilmington.

How to get there: From I-87 north, take exit 30, then NY 73, and drive 28 miles to Lake Placid. Then take NY 86 east 9 miles to Whiteface. From I-87 south, take exit 34, then NY 9N west 16 miles to NY 86. Take NY 86 for 3 miles to Whiteface.

Total miles of biking available: 25+

The lift: You ride to midmountain on a double chairlift; your bike goes up on a separate chair on a removable rack. As you head up the hill you can see the Summit House and the New York State weather observatory on top of the 4867-foot peak, accessible via a toll road in summer. As you pass tower #10, you can see the finish building and the scoreboard used for the downhill and giant slalom events during the 1980 Winter Olympics. Between towers #10 and #15, you can hear the water rushing down Stag Brook, and as you near tower #15 you can see Stag Brook Falls. There is a hiking trail that parallels the brook, but mountain bikes are not allowed. As you near tower #18, you'll see the wooden bridge that was part of the women's downhill event.

After 18 minutes on the same lift that carried Ingemar Stenmark and the Mahre brothers, you reach the top of the lift at 2125 feet.

At the midstation lodge there are rest rooms and a snack bar. Throughout the resort, you leave your bike in racks that utilize old tires from the lift pulleys.

Season and hours: Whiteface is open to mountain bikers from mid-June through Columbus Day weekend, 9 AM–4 PM.

Prices: A ride on the chairlift costs $8 ($6 junior) for one trip or $15 ($10 junior) for the day. A trail pass is $5 ($3 junior).

Rental bikes: Bike rentals range from $8 per hour for a standard mountain bike to $30 a day for a full-suspension bike.

Bike shop: The shop at the mountain has some parts, but for full service try Mountain Run (518-523-9443), 359 Main Street, Lake Placid.

Trail identification: Trails are marked by either white signs with a blue bike logo and lettering or white signs with black lettering.

Special features: Two chairlifts take you to 3676-foot Little Whiteface and allow you to experience the longest vertical descent in the East, 2500 feet.

Reservation number: 518-946-2223

Internet address: http://www.lakeplacid.com/olypcsum.shtml

Hiking: Hikers have access to the entire mountain, but the only trail open exclusively to hikers is the Stag Brook Falls trail. Guided tours are available daily at 2 PM at the midstation lodge.

Other activities: The 1980 Olympic Nordic events were held at the Mount Van Hoevenberg area (518-523-3764 or http://www.lakeplacid.com/olypcsum.shtml#vanho), 15 miles south of Whiteface on NY 86 and NY 73. Also operated by the Olympic Regional Development Committee, it features almost 30 miles of cross-country trails, more suitable for children and beginners than is Whiteface. It's open 9 AM–5 PM daily from late June to mid-October. Trail passes are $5 for adults (juniors $2).

The Lake Placid area hosted both the 1932 and the 1980 Winter Olympics; visitors can take a chairlift ride to the top of the Olympic ski jumping tower. At the Kodak Sports Park you can watch ski jumpers perform aerial stunts, landing in a pool of water. At the Mount Van Hoevenberg Olympic Sports Complex, ride to the top of the bobsled run—you can even experience a ride down on a wheeled bobsled. Tour the Olympic Ice Stadium; admission includes a visit to the Winter Olympics Museum. And you can drive your car to the top of the Whiteface Mountain Veterans Memorial Highway. Eastman Kodak offers a package that includes admission to all of the above activities.

The abolitionist John Brown moved to East Elba, near

Lake Placid, in 1849. He came here to help free blacks form an agricultural community, to be called Timbucto. He is buried here, near the restored farmhouse, along with two of his sons and several followers. The John Brown Historic Site is open late May to late October, Wednesday through Saturday, 10 AM–5 PM, Sundays and holidays 1–5 PM.

Festivals: Typical summer activities are a Native American festival in August and an Oktoberfest the first weekend of October.

Campgrounds: Whiteface KOA (518-946-7878 or 1-800-562-0368) in Wilmington has 190 sites; North Pole Campground (518-946-7733 or 1-800-245-0228) in Wilmington has 82 sites; Wilmington Notch (518-946-7172), 4 miles west on NY 86, has 54 sites.

Suggested itinerary

You may want to start out with a ride down the roads and singletracks of Whiteface's easiest run:

Whiteface Trip 1: #1 Easy Way

Distance: 1.83 miles
Terrain: Ski-area access roads and trails
Difficulty: Moderate
Time: 11 minutes
Elevation loss: 880 feet

0.00   After leaving the chairlift, go right and then immediately veer to the right at the Y.

0.05   Just before the midmountain lodge, by the STAG BROOK FALLS NATURE TRAIL sign, go left onto the trail signed #1 EASY WAY and #2 AUTOBAHN.

0.09   By the entrance to the nature trail, signed NO BIKES, veer right and ride through a section of a racecourse, then descend on the trail that parallels the trees lining Stag Brook.

34

0.37   *Where Trail #4 continues straight, you go left onto Trail #1. You'll encounter a steep descent, then a short, steep climb.*

0.46   *After riding under the main lift, cross Stag Brook and briefly descend on an unsigned rocky road.*

0.63   *After losing 410 feet in 5 minutes, you'll arrive at the junctions of Trails #2, #15, and #16. Veer right and descend on an unsigned work road, shared by Trails #1 and #2. At a Y, Trail #1 goes left after a very sandy section. At the bottom of the Bunny Hutch lift, go right and descend on a paved road.*

1.83   *You return to the main lodge.*

For something different, how about a blast down the dirt roads of:

Whiteface Trip 2: #2 Autobahn

Distance: *1.86 miles*
Terrain: *Ski-area access roads and trails*
Difficulty: *Moderate*
Time: *15 minutes*
Elevation loss: *870 feet*

0.00   *After leaving the chairlift, go right and then immediately left at the Y onto #2 Autobahn, an extremely rocky dirt road that soon crosses Stag Brook.*

0.79   *After dropping 520 feet in 7 minutes, you arrive at a junction with #1 Easy Way. Continue to the right on Trail #2 and cross Stag Brook once again. Soon you pass the scoreboard for the Olympic Downhill and Giant Slalom events. Then the road enters the shelter of some trees and Trail #2 veers to the right, leaving the trees.*

1.72   *You have your choice of staying on the road or descending on a slalom course that includes a jump.*

1.88   *You're back at the lodge.*

After a snack or meal from the lodge's café—you can eat outside while sitting on the deck—how about some singletracks on the southern slopes:

Whiteface Trip 3: #4 Burton's Blvd.

Distance: 1.29 miles
Terrain: Ski-area access roads and trails
Difficulty: Moderate
Time: 12 minutes
Elevation loss: 830 feet

0.0   After leaving the chairlift, go right and then immediately veer to the right at the Y. Just before the midmountain lodge, by the STAG BROOK FALLS NATURE TRAIL sign, go left onto the trail signed #1 EASY WAY and #2 AUTOBAHN.

0.09   By the entrance to the nature trail signed NO BIKES, veer right and ride through a part of a racecourse, then descend on the trail that parallels the trees lining Stag Brook.

0.36   Where Trail #1 goes left, keep to the right on #4 Burton's Blvd., on which you soon encounter a series of steep switchbacks. After you ride by the Olympic finish line sign, go right onto a dirt road, Trail #2.

0.70   You leave the road and go right onto #9 Bear, a singletrack through a meadow that veers left where Trail #8 takes off to the right. Then, at a T, you veer left onto a trail by a tree with a #7 sign. Where the trail climbs, you go right and descend through a meadow.

1.16   Go left onto a dirt road, which is unsigned Trail #2.

1.29   Now you're back at the lodge.

If you want to ride some singletracks on both the southern and northern slopes of Whiteface, try:

Professional racers compete in a cross-country event.

Whiteface Trip 4: #12 Reservoir Run

Distance: *1.56 miles*
Terrain: *Ski-area access roads and trails*
Difficulty: *Moderate*
Time: *19 minutes*
Elevation loss: *930 feet*
Elevation gain: *40 feet*

0.0   *After leaving the chairlift, go right and immediately veer to the right at the Y. Then veer to the right of the midmountain lodge and ride past the Little Whiteface lift onto Trail #3 to begin a short, steep climb. At the top of the climb, you go into woods to the left.*

After riding through an area over exposed granite ledges, descend through a meadow of wildflowers, from which you have an excellent view into the valley.

0.45   *Carry your bike over snowmaking pipes and enter the woods of* maple, small pines, and ferns on a singletrack. You'll soon encounter a short climb. You exit the woods at a T and go right onto unsigned Trail #4 for the descent.

0.66 Trail #4 merges with Trail #1 and goes to the right.

0.70 After descending 340 feet in 10 minutes, where Trail #1 goes left, you stay straight on Trail #4.

0.89 Where Trail #4 starts to switchback across a meadow, go straight onto #5 Stag Brook Junction.

0.95 After crossing under the main lift, enter the woods on a muddy singletrack and, next to a picnic table, encounter a rocky crossing of Stag Brook. You may want to carry your bike over the brook. Emerging from woods, turn right onto a dirt road, unsigned Trail #2. Almost immediately you leave the road, turning left onto Trail #14. Then where Trail #14 goes right, stay straight onto #13 The Medalist.

1.22 Go right back into the woods on #12 Reservoir Run, a singletrack, and veer left onto an unsigned trail. Trail #12 then immediately goes to the right again. You emerge from the trees and descend on a ski run toward the lodge.

1.56 You're back at the lodge.

3
Plattekill, New York

I've mountain biked in the rugged San Gabriel Mountains, the Rockies, the Green Mountains, the White Mountains, the Laurentians, and the Adirondacks. But the Catskills? Before I visited, I was expecting Plattekill to offer rather tame mountain biking. Once I tried it, however, I realized why it's often referred to as Splatterkill!

As I waited in the lodge to get my lift ticket I began to feel uneasy. I overheard fragments of conversation about broken helmets, lacerations, and stitches. The young woman selling the tickets seemed to be in pain when she walked, and she was sitting in a wheelchair, "just because it's comfortable," she assured me. Finally, I noticed that most of the cyclists were wearing Kevlar body armor; this is the only resort I visited for this book that rents full-face downhill helmets and body armor. As if that weren't clue enough, I could tell from the various pierced body parts on display that this is serious downhill territory. But if you've never tried downhill mountain biking, don't be frightened away. Although it obviously has trails that appeal to the most hard-core cyclist, the beginning runs at Plattekill are among the easiest in this book.

Plattekill is a small resort near Roxbury; the "kill" in Plattekill doesn't refer to the fate of mountain bikers, but rather reflects the area's Dutch heritage ("kil" means "creek"). This is "upstate" New York, a world apart from the glitter of Manhattan or the charms of the Hudson Valley. Located in the heart of the

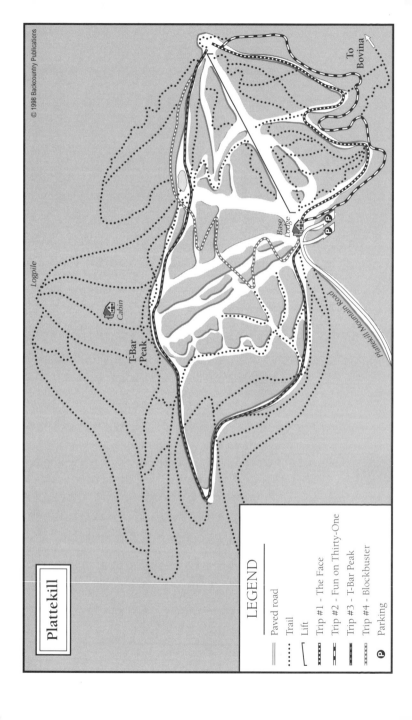

Plattekill

© 1998 Backcountry Publications

Logpile

T-Bar Peak

Cabin

Base Lodge

Plattekill Mountain Road

To Bovina

LEGEND

═══	Paved road
⋯⋯⋯	Trail
⌐⌐⌐	Lift
▮▮▮	Trip #1 - The Face
▮▮▮	Trip #2 - Fun on Thirty-One
▮▮▮	Trip #3 - T-Bar Peak
▮▮▮	Trip #4 - Blockbuster
P	Parking

Catskills, Plattekill is nevertheless only 2¹/₂ hours north of the city, making it the closest resort to metropolitan New York that offers downhill mountain biking. It's also the only lift-accessed mountain biking in New York State that takes you to the actual summit of the mountain. At Plattekill, mountain biking is the main attraction in the summer. As the resort has neither golf course, tennis courts, nor shops, most visitors come here in search of serious downhill riding.

Roxbury claims two famous native sons. The impressive Jay Gould Memorial Reformed Church was built by the railroad magnate's children in 1892 out of rock, wood, and stained glass. Sunday morning servics are open to the public, but I doubt many hard-core cyclists will be drawn away from the runs. Another native was the naturalist John Burroughs, the author of 23 books. Visitors to his Roxbury cabin included Henry Ford, Thomas Edison, John Muir, and Teddy Roosevelt. Roxbury's John Burroughs Memorial is open weekends July 4 through Labor Day, 11 AM–5 PM.

How to get there: From New York City, take the New York State Thruway, I-87, to Exit 19, Kingston. From the traffic rotary at Kingston, go west on NY 28 for approximately 45 miles to Arkville. At Arkville, just before the railroad crossing, turn right at Crosby's Farm Equipment. After one mile turn right onto NY 30 North. After 5 miles turn left onto Cold Spring Road; follow the yellow signs for 4 miles to Plattekill.

From Albany take I-90 West to I-88 south. At Exit 23 take NY 30 South to Roxbury. Turn right onto Bridge Street, go 100 yards, cross a small bridge, and bear left onto Plattekill Mountain Road for 4 miles to the resort.

From the west take I-88 to Exit 13, Oneonta. Take NY 23 East to Grand Gorge. Turn right onto NY 30 South to Roxbury. In Roxbury, turn right onto Bridge Street, go 100 yards,

Hard-core cyclists wear full-body armor at Plattekill.

cross a small bridge, and bear left onto Plattekill Mountain Road. Follow it for 4 miles to the resort.

Total miles of biking available: 61

The lift: Before you're allowed to purchase your lift ticket, you must watch a five-minute video on safety. The staff at Plattekill keeps a signed copy of your liability waiver on file, so that on subsequent visits you can just initial and date it.

The Plattekill chair could be known as "the Fastest Lift in the East." The triple chair whisks you 850 vertical feet to the top in $6^1/2$ minutes. There's a lift attendant at the bottom, but just to load your bike; you're on your own to get onto the swiftly moving chair. At the top, the lift attendant doesn't swing the chair out of the way to keep it from hitting you as you get off; he's only there to remove the bikes. To dismount, you must jump off the chair and run down a small incline to get out of its path.

Season and hours: Plattekill is open weekends and holidays, May through October, 10 AM–5 PM.

Prices: An all-day lift ticket is $18; a trail pass is $10.

Rental bikes: A bike with front suspension is $30 per day; a full-suspension bike is $40. Helmets, knee pads, and elbow pads are $5 each per day. Body armor is $15 per day. A beginner's package, consisting of an all-day lift ticket, bike, helmet rental, 1-hour lesson, and guide, is $55. Lessons and guided tours are $10 per hour.

Bike shop: Plattekill features a full-service pro shop.

Trail identification: Trails are well marked with numbered signs.

Special features: Plattekill features child care, a cafeteria, and a bar. Night riding is featured on selected Saturday nights throughout the season; bike lights are required, and can be rented at the resort.

Reservations: 1-800-GOTTA-BIKE, or 1-800-468-8224.

Internet address: http://www.westchesterweb.com/plattekill/BIKEPLAT.HTML

E-mail address: plattekill@aol.com

Hiking: A single ride up the chairlift is $5. Plattekill certainly offers some nice hiking, but the mountain bikers rule here. I'd either stick to the left side of the main lift or I'd hike some of the interesting local features, such as Vroman's Nose, near Middleburgh on NY 30. A description of this and other local hikes can be found on the Internet at: http://www.aspenserv.com/hiking/hudson.html

Riders' comments: "I have been to Plattekill four times this summer. Plattekill is, in a word, AWESOME! It is super technical, with lots of loose shale. It is really hard on equipment (the bike's and yours) so be prepared!"

Other attractions: In a typical season Plattekill features 10 weekends of NORBA mountain bike racing. In March, Plattekill has mountain bike races on the snow. Although the resort itself has no golf course, they can be found throughout the area. The Catskills have numerous antique stores, B&Bs, and restaurants. I'd love to tour Route 30 on a bike, stopping at every hamlet and historical marker. The Woodstock Guild (914-679-2079) in Woodstock features musical and dance presentations. The Belleayre Music Festival (800-942-6904) in Highmount presents musical performances during the summer and fall. If you like old trains, go for a ride on the Delaware & Ulster Rail Ride (914-586-DURR) on NY 28.

Campgrounds: Plattekill is one of the few resort areas in this book to offer on-site camping. The primitive camping costs $5 per tent and $10 per camper.

Suggested itinerary

For your first ride try an easy cruise back to the lodge:

Plattekill Trip 1: The Face

Distance: *3.22 miles*
Terrain: *Ski-area access roads and trails*
Difficulty: *Moderate*
Time: *30 Minutes*
Elevation loss: *840 feet*

0.00   *After leaving the lift, turn right and begin descending Trail 30.*

2.61   *Go left (stay on Trail 30) at the hairpin where unmarked Trail 55 goes straight ahead. This gradual descent takes you to a trail junction; go to the right over the bridge.*

This is a good spot to watch the more aggressive riders take about a 3-foot jump as they descend Trail 31.

3.22   *After descending 840 feet in 30 minutes you're back at the lodge.*

If you're ready for another moderate run try:

Plattekill Trip 2: Fun on Thirty-One

Distance: *1.43 miles*
Terrain: *Ski-area access roads and trails*
Difficulty: *Moderate*
Time: *20 minutes*
Elevation loss: *120 feet*

0.00 *After getting off the lift, begin your descent on Trail 30.*

0.07 *Almost immediately turn left onto Trail 31.*

You'll encounter several places where the trail divides, but all options seem to end up back on the main trail.

0.96 *Veer left before the bridge to stay on Trail 31.*

1.43 *After descending 810 feet in 20 minutes, you're back at the start.*

Now you may be ready to explore the other side of the resort on a ride that involves a little climbing:

Plattekill Trip 3: T-Bar Peak

Distance: *2.07 miles*
Terrain: *Ski-area access roads and trails*
Difficulty: *Moderate*
Time: *35 minutes*
Elevation loss: *1030 feet*
Elevation gain: *210 feet*

0.00 *After getting off the lift go left onto Trail 21.*

0.33 *After dropping 120 feet, at the spot where Trail 23 goes left, keep climbing to the right onto unmarked Trail 13.*

0.75 *After a 10-minute climb, a walker in places for me, you'll reach 3350-foot T-Bar Peak.*

From this perspective you can see the patchwork quilt of

farms in the Platteville Valley below.

Descend on Trail 16, an easy descent on a grassy ski run.

2.07 *After descending 1030 feet in 35 minutes, you're back at the lift again.*

Now you're ready for something a little more challenging:

Plattekill Trip 4: Blockbuster

Distance: *1.44 miles*
Terrain: *Ski-area access roads and trails*
Difficulty: *Difficult*
Time: *20 minutes*
Elevation loss: *950 feet*

0.00 *After getting off the lift, turn left onto Trail 21.*

0.07 *Veer left onto Trail 1 and ride straight ahead.*

0.38 *After dropping 130 feet, go left onto Blockbuster, where Trail 13 is straight ahead. After a short, steep descent, which offers a great view of the base lodge, go right onto a rocky singletrack.*

0.55 *Make a sharp left turn and begin a steep descent toward the lodge.*

0.94 *After descending 590 feet, turn right onto a singletrack into the woods.*

1.03 *Leave the singletrack and turn left onto an easier trail; then turn right and begin descending a ski run; then go to the right back into the woods on another singletrack.*

This trail is extremely technical; I encountered a couple of drops that were too steep for my bike and were even challenging to walk down.

1.24 *I bail out and go left onto an easier trail.*

1.44 *After dropping 950 feet in 40 minutes I'm back at the lodge and ready for a break.*

4
Jiminy Peak, Massachusetts

Jiminy Peak looks good on paper: located near the Central Berkshire town of Hancock, it's not that far from New York City or Boston; it has lift-accessed mountain biking at a resort that also features an alpine slide, miniature golf, Frisbee golf, and other attractions for the family. And although its Web page shows mountain biking, Jiminy's recorded phone message doesn't mention it. Perhaps that should have been my clue.

From the highway, Jiminy appeared to be closed; only the sign ALPINE SLIDE OPEN told me otherwise. And the alpine slide is king at Jiminy. In fact, the average age of the visitor to Jiminy in summer is so young that a 20-year-old will probably feel ancient.

Jiminy's runs are all intermediate to advanced; there's no way for the beginning mountain biker to taste the sport. And even if the casual visitor wants to give it a try, there are no rental bikes available.

For the more advanced mountain biker it's a bargain, although there are no marked trails and none of the personnel at the top of the lift could direct me to runs indicated on the excellent trail map.

On the plus side, it's a resort where a skilled mountain biker could enjoy a few hours of downhilling while younger members of the family take advantage of the other attractions.

It's too bad that Jiminy Peak lags behind other ski areas that

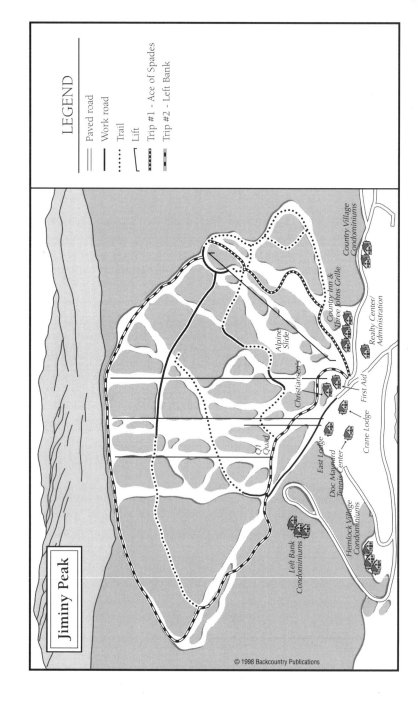

Jiminy Peak

LEGEND

- ═══ Paved road
- ━━━ Work road
- ⋯⋯ Trail
- ⌐ Lift
- ▓▓▓ Trip #1 - Ace of Spades
- ▥▥▥ Trip #2 - Left Bank

Alpine Slide

Christiansen's

Quad

East Lodge

Doc Maynard Tennis Center

Left Bank Condominiums

Hemlock Village Condominiums

Crane Lodge

First Aid

Realty Center/ Administration

Country Inn & Three Johns Grille

Country Village Condominiums

© 1998 Backcountry Publications

promote mountain biking, because Western Massachusetts was the site of some of the earliest skiing and ski resort innovations in the Northeast. Nearby Mount Greylock, at 3491 feet the highest point in Massachusetts, had two trails cut by Civilian Conservation Corps crews during the Depression. Six thousand spectators watched a German team from the University of Munich beat Dartmouth at the 1938 Eastern Downhill Championships on Greylock's Thunderbolt trail.

The Berkshires also had ski trains that brought skiers from New York City for $2 round-trip and featured early tow ropes, for which skiers were charged $1.50. In those early days the trails were sometimes groomed in summer by goats.

Brodie, around the corner from Jiminy, was another early resort. When its founder died in 1950, it was taken over by Walter Schoenknecht. He lost money at Brodie, but acquired the skills that allowed him to make Mount Snow (see chapter 5) a success.

How to get there: From the Mass Pike, I-90, take US 7 north 20 miles. Follow the signs 3 miles west to Jiminy Peak. From the north, take US 7 for 10 miles south from Williamstown. Follow the signs 3 miles to Jiminy Peak.

Total miles of biking available: 15

The lift: The lift is an old double chairlift that takes 12 minutes to carry you halfway up the mountain. It's primarily for carrying the sleds and riders for the alpine slide. The bike is carried on a rack designed to hold the sleds, and as a precaution your bike is held on by both gravity and a bungee cord. As you ride up between maples, birch, and ash, you'll see wildflowers and wild strawberries in the meadow below.

Season and hours: Memorial Day weekend through Labor Day weekend, 10 AM–4 PM.

Prices: A booklet good for five rides is $13. There is no fee to

The author's end-of-summer collection of lift tickets

use the trails without taking the lift.

Rental bikes: None

Bike shop: None

Trail identification: None

Special features: Alpine slide, infrared skeet shooting range, Frisbee golf, tennis, trout pond, miniature golf. The hotel next to the lift has an enticing pool, but it's only available for hotel guests. However, day visitors can use a pool over by the tennis center.

Reservation number: 1-413-738-SNOW

Internet address: http://www.jiminypeak.com/fun.html

E-mail address: info@jiminypeak.com

Hiking: You can hike the trails of Jiminy without a trail fee. The trails of Mount Greylock, which includes the Appalachian Trail, are only a few minutes away.

Other attractions: Jiminy hosts the 24 Hours of New England marathon mountain bike race in August.

Williamstown, Massachusetts, 10 miles to the north, is the home of Williams College, which holds a theater festival every summer. Williamstown was also the home of Sterling and Francine Clark. The beneficiaries of the Singer Sewing Machine fortune, they spent their lives collecting art, especially the works of French impressionists. Today, their former home is the Sterling and Francine Clark Art Institute; admission is free.

Campground: Brodie Mountain, a mile north on US 7, has 150 sites, showers, and a pool.

Hostel: The Appalachian Mountain Club (413-443-0011 or http://www.outdoors.org/Lodging/Mass/) operates the rustic Bascom Lodge, an excellent hostel offering overnight accommodations and meals from May to mid-October, on the summit of Greylock.

Suggested itinerary

For your first ride, try Ace of Spades:

Jiminy Trip 1: Ace of Spades

Distance: *0.64 mile*
Terrain: *Downhill ski run*
Difficulty: *Moderate to difficult*
Time: *8 minutes*
Elevation loss: *600 feet*

0.00   *After getting off the lift and retrieving your bike from the operator, go right and head toward the start of the alpine slide. Descend on Ace of Spades, a ski run that goes to the left of the slide.*

This is a fairly steep run, with no markers or signs. At any of the more popular resorts, the way down would be marked by the erosion caused by previous bikes. But I found my way by following the tracks in the unmowed grass of an ATV that had gone up earlier in the morning. I took my time, because the high grasses made it hard to see holes, rocks, or water bars.

0.64   *In 8 minutes you're back at the base.*

Jiminy's mountain bike trail map says the road to the top requires a cyclist in "excellent aerobic condition." A challenge if I ever saw one:

Jiminy Trip 2: Left Bank

Distance: *2.13 miles*
Terrain: *Ski-area work roads*
Difficulty: *Moderate to difficult*
Time: *30 minutes*
Elevation gain: *500 feet*
Elevation loss: *1140 feet*

0.00   *From the top of the lift, you go left and then immediately begin climbing a steep dirt road, which offers views back into Jericho, the valley that Jiminy overlooks.*

For me, this first part was a walker.

0.09   *The trail to the right looks like it would lead to a view, but it's only of a snowmaking pond.*

0.28   *After 7 minutes, by the* WEST WAY *and* NORTH GLADES *signs, a flat section allows nice northerly views into the Jericho Valley.*

0.47   *Veer left toward the Upper Liftline lift.*

0.53   *A 12-minute climb rewards you with nice views of farmland down in the Jericho Valley. You begin your descent by going between the* UPPER LIFTLINE *and* LEFT BANK *signs.*

0.66   *Go left by the* WHIRLAWAY *sign and enjoy an excellent view of the*

Berkshires to the east, including the top of Mount Greylock.

This is a tough descent, especially on an old hard-tailed Specialized, and the surface is a very loose dirt. This is common in the West, but Jiminy is the only place I've seen it in the Northeast.

1.30   Take in the good views of the resort and then veer left by the WINDING BROOK sign.

1.67   Veer left at the QUAD CHAIR sign and begin heading toward the lodge buildings.

1.97   Pass a lift, then veer right toward the lodge.

It's a good thing the shotguns at the skeet range are infrared, because you ride directly in front of them.

2.13   After 30 minutes of biking, you're back at the lift.

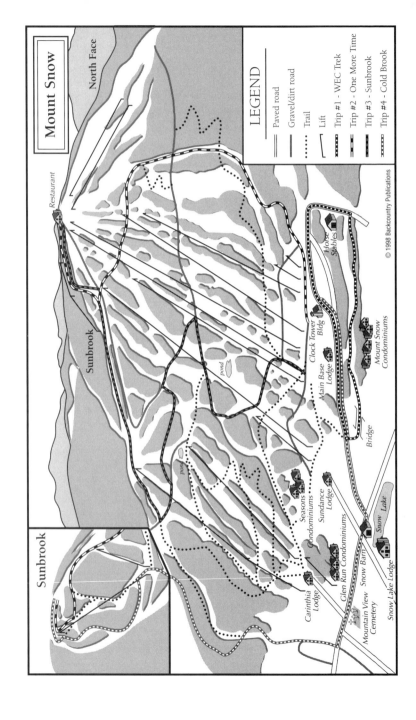

Mount Snow

North Face

Restaurant

Sunbrook

Sunbrook

Horse
Stables

Clock Tower
Bldg

Main Base
Lodge

Mount Snow
Condominiums

pond

pond

Bridge

Seasons
Condominiums

Sundance
Lodge

Carinthia
Lodge

Glen Run Condominiums

Snow Barn

Mountain View
Cemetery

Snow Lake

Snow Lake Lodge

LEGEND

Paved road
Gravel/dirt road
Trail
Lift
Trip #1 - WEC Trek
Trip #2 - One More Time
Trip #3 - Sunbrook
Trip #4 - Cold Brook

© 1998 Backcountry Publications

5
Mount Snow, Vermont

Mount Snow has it all: excellent views; descents from moderate to extreme, singletracks, and great cross-country trails; condos with outstanding views of the mountain; Mountain Bike Schools for teenagers and adults and Mountain Bike Camps for children; and in the evening you can enjoy a movie, a great meal, or live entertainment: Movies and restaurants are in Dover or nearby Wilmington. Except on race weekends, there are no nearby campgrounds.

Mount Snow is located in the town of Dover, which was incorporated on October 30, 1810. (Before that it had been a part of Wardsboro.) Dover was apparently named after the British town on the English Channel.

There used to be a small strip of land that first belonged to Somerset and then to Wilmington. On the map, it looked like a leg or handle jutting out from Wilmington; thus it was called the Wilmington Leg, the Wilmington Handle, or just the Handle. Although Dover acquired the land in 1869, the name stuck, and the road that parallels VT 100 and connects Mount Snow with Mount Haystack is today known as Handle Road.

Walter Schoenknecht, the resort's first developer, bought the land in 1953 from Reuben Snow and named the resort and the 3605-foot peak (originally called Somerset Mountain and later Mount Pisgah) after him. Mount Snow opened for skiing in 1954 and prospered into the 1960s. But the fuel shortages of the 1970s caused skiers to stay away. In 1977, Mount Snow was purchased by the owners of Killington. The current operators, the American Skiing Company, also operate Haystack, Killington/Pico, and Sugarbush in Vermont; Attitash Bear in New Hampshire; and Sugarloaf and Sunday River in Maine.

How to get there: From the east, take I-91 to exit 2. Take VT 9 west 20 miles to Wilmington. At the signal, go right on VT 100 north; 9 miles to Mount Snow.

From Bennington, take VT 9 east 21 miles to Wilmington. Go left at the signal onto VT 100 north 9 miles to Mount Snow.

Total miles of biking available: 140+

The lift: The lift operates Thursday through Monday. As you take one chairlift to the top, your bike rides up on a removable rack on the back of another chair, usually the one in front of you.

On your 22-minute ride to the top, you can see from the lift the hills to the east of Dover, including Mount Monadnock in New Hampshire; south to Mount Holyoke in Massachusetts; and Somerset Lake and Killington to the north.

Season and hours: Mount Snow is open from Memorial Day weekend through Columbus Day weekend, 9 AM–4 PM.

Prices: At Mount Snow, a lift ticket costs $8 for one trip to the top; $27 for an all-day pass. Before you can take the lift, you must watch a 5-minute video on mountain bike safety, something all resorts should require.

Rental bikes: Bikes are $30 for a full day, $25 for 4 hours, and $20 for 2 hours.

Bike shop: Mount Snow has a pro shop that services and sells bikes and accessories.

Trail identification: Bike trails are marked with yellow diamonds with red numbers or arrows. Hiking trails are identified by white squares with green numbers, arrows, and a hiking logo.

Special features: The Summit Lodge offers snacks and meals from Mount Snow's 3605-foot summit. Trails vary from easy access roads to technical singletracks. If your bike is filthy from the mud and water, you can wash it off with the hose (part of the snowmaking equipment in winter) at the base.

Mount Snow also features a Mountain Bike School. Founded in 1988, this $132 course is offered on summer weekends from Memorial Day through Columbus Day. It includes use of the lifts, trail-access passes, lunch each day, a Saturday-afternoon party, use of a helmet, and 12 hours of instruction and riding. You'll learn shifting, braking, weight distribution, cadence, ascending, and descending.

For parents who want to ride, Mount Snow offers day-care and camping programs for youngsters 6 weeks to 12 years of age. Plus, there is a playground right in front of the lodge.

Mount Snow has hosted the annual Grundig/UCI Mountain Bike World Cup, the mountain biking portion of the ESPN Extreme Games, and the Vermont State Dual Slalom Championships.

In late winter or early spring, Mount Snow has a mountain bike race down the still-snow-covered skiing slalom course.

Reservation number: 1-800-245-SNOW

Internet address: http://www.mountsnow.com/summer/biking.html

E-mail address: mtsnow@sover.net

Hiking: Mount Snow features the Merrell Hiking Center, the starting point for more than 20 miles of trails. A trail map and pocket field guide are $5. For $10 you can get the map, the pocket field guide, and a chairlift ride. You can even rent a pair of Merrell hiking boots.

Other activities: Biking-oriented weekends include the Extreme Tour, the Inn-to-Inn Tour, the Family Weekend, the

Wilderness Weekend, and the Women's Weekend. For the golfer, Mount Snow has its own course, but a more breathtaking course is a few miles to the south at Haystack. I'm not a golfer, but I've seen the 11th hole there while cycling along Mann Road, and it's almost enough to make me want to take up the sport. Wayne Mills in the *Brattleboro Reformer* described the 11th hole at Haystack as "one of the most spectacular and fun holes I've ever played . . . You feel like you're launching your golf ball off the earth." The town of Dover offers shopping, dining, and movies. Nearby Wilmington features dining and shopping.

At Harriman Reservoir, 2.5 miles west of Wilmington on VT 9, you can rent a Surfbike from Green Mountain Flagships (802-464-2975). This is a single-hull, pedal-powered boat, essentially a bicycle that you can ride on the water. It's as different from the old paddleboats as a mountain bike is from a 1950s three-speed.

Other attractions: Typical events in summer might include the Southern Vermont Highland Games, the Green Mountain Irish Games, the Vermont Open Chili Cookoff, the Fall Foliage Crafts Fair, and the Brewer's Fest.

Campgrounds: Molly Stark State Park (802-464-5460), a few miles west of Wilmington on VT 9, has 34 campsites. Jamaica State Park (802-874-4600) on VT 30 has 57 campsites. The Grout Pond Recreation Area (802-362-2307) in Wardsboro has 5 campsites.

On race weekends, one of Mount Snow's parking lots is converted into a campground.

Suggested itinerary

Before taking the lift to the top, you may want to warm up by riding a short trail—including log crossings, mud, rocks, stream crossings, short, steep climbs, and short, steep descents—which begins at the parking lot:

Mount Snow Trip 1: WEC Trek

Distance: *1.11 miles*
Terrain: *Cross-country ski trails, dirt roads, and paved roads*
Difficulty: *Easy*
Map: *Mount Snow*
How to get there: *This ride starts from the small parking lot next to Mount Snow's Vacation Center, the building with the clock tower.*
Time: *11 minutes*
Elevation gain: *60 feet*

0.0   Ride out of the parking lot next to the Vacation Center, and turn right onto the one-way road into the main parking lot.

0.06   At the stop sign, turn right and continue riding through the parking lot on the paved road following the signs to SUNDANCE, CARINTHIA, and HAYSTACK base lodges.

0.25   At the bottom of the 50-foot descent, with Snow Lake directly ahead—just before a LOT E sign—you leave the paved road and go left onto a trail toward a wooden bridge.

0.30   Cross the bridge and immediately turn left onto Trail 11, a singletrack into the woods with a stream to the left and condos to the right.

You'll encounter a short, steep descent to the level of the streambed, cross the stream, and ride through a cool, lush area dominated by ferns, then cross a fallen log.

Cross another stream, which has beautiful falls to the left, exit the woods, and go left onto the paved parking lot access road.

1.11   You're back at the start, warmed up and ready to take the lift to the summit.

For a moderate descent that includes steep dirt roads and moderately technical singletracks, with views from Mount Monadnock in New Hampshire to Mount Holyoke, in Massachusetts's Connecticut River Valley, try:

Mount Snow Trip 2: One More Time

Distance: *2.72 miles*
Terrain: *Ski-area access roads and trails*
Difficulty: *Moderate*
Map: *Mount Snow*
Time: *35 minutes*
Elevation loss: *1520 feet*

0.00   *After you leave the lift, follow the* TRAILS *1, 2, 3 signs next to the Summit Lodge.*

0.01   *Follow the* TRAIL *1 sign and veer to the right of the building with the summit map sign.*

0.15   *By Sunbrook Lift 19, go left at the junction following Trail 2 and Trail 3 and descend directly under Lift 19.*

0.40   *At lift tower 14, having dropped 200 feet, you follow Trail 1, climb slightly, enter the woods, and ride through a muddy technical area with several bridges/boardwalks.*

0.72   *After another difficult area, you leave the woods and stay straight on Trail 12.*

   You'll cross a gravel work road, and—with Mount Monadnock straight ahead—enter the woods to the left and traverse several ski runs.

1.09   *After 15 minutes and a descent of 300 feet, cross under the main Summit lift and descend under the Standard lift. With the Somerset Reservoir straight ahead, turn right and descend through another difficult section.*

1.59   *With Mount Monadnock straight ahead at the junction with Trail 13, you go left down the One More Time ski run.*

In early spring Mount Snow holds bike races down its snow-covered slalom course.

2.00 *Cross a singletrack, Trail 7, and continue descending.*

This is a tricky, steep section that turns into a very pleasant, easy, singletrack descent.

2.26 *Merge with Hiking Trail 5, then go left into the woods.*

2.72 *You're back at the main lodge.*

Now, for a trip that allows you to cruise more of the dirt roads and explore more of the singletracks that Mount Snow has cut through the woods, try:

Mount Snow Trip 3: Sunbrook

Distance: *3.57 miles*
Terrain: *Ski-area access roads and trails*
Difficulty: *Moderate*
Map: *Mount Snow*
Time: *45 minutes*

Elevation loss: *1560 feet*

0.00 *After you leave the lift, follow the* TRAILS *1, 2, 3 signs next to the Summit Lodge. You may want to take the time to have a snack in the lodge.*

0.01 *Follow the* TRAIL *1 sign and veer to the right of the building with the summit map sign.*

0.15 *At Sunbrook Lift 19, by the junction with Trail 2, go straight onto Trail 1, which soon enters the woods on a singletrack.*

0.84 *After dropping 260 feet in 15 minutes, at the junction with Trail 12 you'll leave the woods and continue to descend on Trail 1.*

1.29 *You reach a gravel work road, closed to downhill biking, and stay on Trail 1, which parallels the work road on the left, then veers to the right and offers a great view of 3165-foot Mount Monadnock.*

1.63 *Trail 1 goes left onto a dirt road by the* TO UPPER MAIN STREET *sign, then you leave the gravel road and veer left into the woods on a singletrack, a steep climb, which is also Hiking Trail 10.*

2.04 *Go right onto a gravel road signed* TRAIL *4 and you'll come immediately to a junction of two gravel roads, where you veer left.*

2.47 *At the T, go right. Then, just past the Sundance Lift, go left onto an unnumbered singletrack and follow the blazes through the woods. Leaving the woods, go right on a dirt road, then immediately turn left, leave the road, and go straight onto a singletrack. Directly under the main lift, you go right. Make another right on a gravel road; then, just past the main lift, veer left.*

3.57 *You're back at the main lodge.*

After a snack in the lodge's café, it's time to explore the southern side of Mount Snow and see the resting place of the man for whom Mount Snow is named:

Mount Snow Trip 4: Cold Brook

Distance: *4.92 miles*
Terrain: *Ski-area access roads and trails*
Difficulty: *Moderate*
Map: *Mount Snow*
Time: *50 minutes*
Elevation loss: *1780 feet*

0.00   *After you leave the lift, follow the* TRAILS *1, 2, 3 signs, next to the Summit Lodge.*

0.01   *Follow the* TRAIL *1 sign and veer to the right of the building with the summit map sign.*

0.15   *By Sunbrook Lift 19, go left at the junction following Trail 2 and Trail 3 and descend directly under Lift 19. Trail 3 veers to the right by the* MOONWALK *sign. You leave the ski run and go left into the woods.*

1.24   *Where Trail 2 climbs, go right and descend into the woods on Trail 14, on which you'll encounter a muddy, difficult descent.*

2.47   *After plunging 1190 feet in 30 minutes, leave the woods and go straight ahead onto Trail 5.*

3.13   *You leave the ski area, turn left onto a gravel road by a private home, and continue to descend. When you reach the* KINGSROAD *sign, go left onto unsigned Handle Road.*

4.10   *Just opposite the Carinthia lift is the Mountain View Cemetery.*

From the road you can spot a grave with the name Jane Snow; further exploration reveals that this cemetery is the final resting place for many of the Snows. Reuben Snow (1893–1953), who sold this land to Walter Schoenknecht, is buried in the northeast corner.

After the stop sign, beyond the cemetery, continue riding through the lower parking lot for Mount Snow.

4.60   In the parking lot, go left onto the road by Snow Lake and climb the steep hill.

4.92 After the steep hill, turn left and you're back at the Main Lodge.

If you have the energy, you may want to consider driving or riding to Mount Snow's cross-country area and experiencing the nice variety of singletracks with stream crossings, dirt roads, and paved roads:

Mount Snow Trip 5: Airport Loop

Distance: *5.84 miles*
Terrain: *Cross-country ski trails, dirt roads, and paved roads*
Difficulty: *Moderate*
Map: *Mount Snow: Airport Loop*
How to get there: *From the Mount Snow Base Lodge, drive or ride 2.3 miles south on Handle Road. Just past the Suntec Forest development, park in the lot on the left of the road by the metal gate signed* ROAD CLOSED TO MOTORIZED TRAFFIC BY ORDER OF DOVER SELECTMEN.
Time: *1 hour*
Elevation gain: *620 feet*

0.00 Ride around the gate onto signed CROSSTOWN RD, *pass a sign identifying the trail as a part of the Hermitage cross-country trail system, and ride by a pond on the right.*

0.18 At a junction marked by a blue cross-country trail diamond, go right. You'll cross several bridges and ride through a muddy area. At the Y, where the Sugar Momma trail goes to the left, you go right onto signed BEAVER TRAIL, *which has roller-coaster-like rolling bumps, the mountain bike equivalent of moguls. Ferns line this section of the trail, which has a stone wall paralleling it on the right. After passing the junction with the signed* TENZIG TRAIL, *you descend to a muddy area at the bottom, then go straight onto the trail signed* THREE GUYS RUNNING.

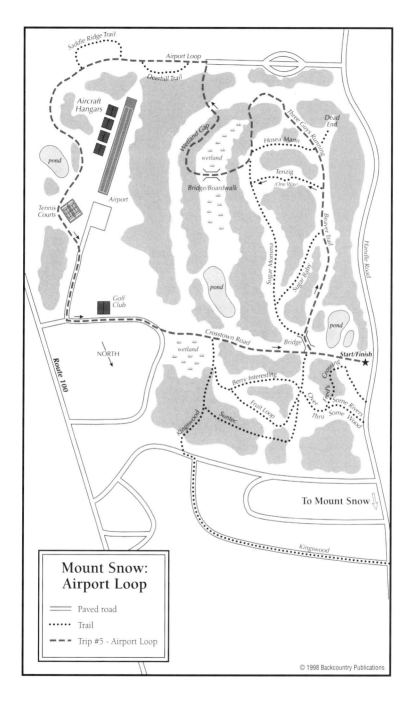

Mount Snow:
Airport Loop

Paved road

.... Trail

— — — Trip #5 - Airport Loop

© 1998 Backcountry Publications

1.28   At the junction with the Sugar Momma Trail, veer right and encounter a very steep descent.

Cross a wetlands on a wooden boardwalk; your bike will make an interesting popping sound as it crosses the planks.

You encounter a steep climb and then turn right where the trail straight ahead is blocked by a TRAIL CLOSED sign.

1.94   After gaining 130 feet in 25 minutes, cross a stream, ride out of the woods, and turn left onto a dirt road. Pass a beaver pond and begin a gradual climb.

2.93   At a three-way junction, take the dirt road to the left. At the junction with some cross-country ski signs, go left, staying on the dirt road, which first descends and then climbs.

3.53   With the main road ahead signed THIS TRAIL OFF LIMITS, go left onto a somewhat technical singletrack trail signed AIRPORT LOOP. You'll emerge from the woods in a meadow next to the hangars of the Mount Snow airport. Go right onto a dirt road that veers to the left between the homes of a housing development. At a T, with the entrance to the airport on your left, go right onto the unsigned dirt road. At the next T, go left onto a paved road and ride past the Mount Snow golf course.

4.77   Where the paved road curves to the right, turn left onto the singletrack signed CROSSTOWN ROAD and ride around another metal gate signed ROAD CLOSED TO MOTORIZED TRAFFIC BY ORDER OF DOVER SELECTMEN.

This is a very fast singletrack with one interesting jump, several huge logs—too large to jump—and a steep descent.

5.84   You are back at the start.

6
Stratton, Vermont

I really want to like the mountain biking experience at Stratton—
Stratton is essentially my "home" resort. I teach snowboarding
there through a school program, and snowboard there more than
at any other resort. But Stratton just doesn't have enough variety
of trails for my tastes. It's not entirely Stratton's fault; attempts to
cut more singletracks are still awaiting Forest Service approval.

On the plus side, the village at Stratton has everything the
visitor may want. Some condos are right in the village. Need a
spare part? The village has at least two pro shops. Hungry? The
village has a variety of restaurants. Plus there are plenty of stores
for the noncyclist. And there's nothing nicer than a summer con-
cert underneath the stars, on Stratton's lower slopes.

The town of Stratton was created by a grant from the New
Hampshire legislature (Vermont was not yet a state) on July 30,
1761. Early settlers came from Cornwall, England, and named
the town here Stratton after a village in southwest England. By
1838 a post office was opened to accommodate the local timber
business.

In those days the town had a population of about 1500. But
in July 1840 more than 15,000 people attended a Whig conven-
tion at Stratton to hear Daniel Webster speak on behalf of the
candidacy of Gen. William Henry Harrison. By 1880, the era of
timber prosperity had ended, and the population declined.

There are almost a dozen peaks in the Stratton area over 2000

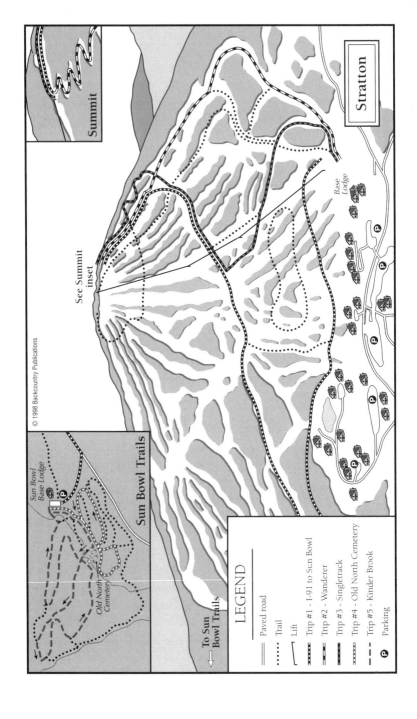

© 1998 Backcountry Publications

Summit

See Summit
inset

Stratton

Base
Lodge

Sun Bowl
Base Lodge

Sun Bowl Trails

Old North
Cemetery

To Sun
Bowl Trails

LEGEND

Paved road

·········· Trail

Lift

Trip #1 - I-91 to Sun Bowl

Trip #2 - Wanderer

Trip #3 - Singletrack

Trip #4 - Old North Cemetery

Trip #5 - Kinder Brook

Ⓟ Parking

feet in height, with 3859-foot Stratton Mountain the tallest. The ideas for two main hiking trails germinated on Stratton's slopes. Benton McKay conceived the idea of the Appalachian Trail while on Stratton's summit. And the idea of the Long Trail connecting Massachusetts and Canada came to James Taylor while he was on its slopes.

Today, as you view the golf course, expensive homes, condos, tennis courts, and shops of Stratton Village, it's hard to imagine that when this resort was planned in the late 1950s, the area was a wilderness—a major obstacle was just the creation of a road between VT 30 and the site of the resort. Many times during the initial 1961–62 season, the access road was impassable because the heavy traffic churned the roads to deep mud.

The opening of the ski resort caused two of the area's most famous citizens to leave. Helen and Scott Nearing had moved to nearby Jamaica, Vermont in the 1950s, in an attempt to "get away from it all" and Helen's books on their experiences helped to fuel the "back to nature" movement of the 1960s and 70s (and indirectly contributed to my relocation to Vermont). But when Stratton's development caused the area to become too crowded, the Nearings left Vermont in 1952 and moved to the coast of Maine.

Today, Stratton is owned by Intrawest, the owners of Mont-Tremblant, in Québec, Canada (see chapter 19).

How to get there: From the east, take I-91 to exit 2. Take VT 9 east to VT 30 and follow that road 35 miles to Bondville. From Bondville, follow the signs 6 miles to Stratton. From Bennington, follow US 7 for 23 miles to VT 30, then take VT 30 for 13 miles to Bondville. From Bondville, follow the signs 6 miles to Stratton.

Total miles of biking available: 30+

The lift: Stratton uses its Starship XII gondola to transport you and your bike inside on the way up to the 3859-foot summit. The gondola runs daily, except Wednesday, from late June through Columbus Day weekend. From the gondola, you can see 3165-foot Mount Monadnock in New Hampshire, 3150-foot Ascutney, the lake formed by Ball Mountain Dam, 4241-foot Killington way out at the northern horizon, Stratton's neighbor 3260-foot Bromley to the northwest, and Stratton's other ski neighbor, 2940-foot Magic Mountain, to the northeast. On a clear day you can see 4867-foot Whiteface to the northwest in New York State and on a very clear day you can make out 6288-foot Mount Washington to the north.

Season and hours: Stratton is open daily from late June to Columbus Day weekend, 9:30 AM–4 PM.

Prices: At Stratton, a ride on the gondola costs $13 for one trip or $20 for an all-day lift ticket ($15 for juniors, 6–12 years old).

Rental bikes: Rates run from $25 per day for a standard mountain bike to $45 for a high-performance bike.

Bike shops: Stratton Sports and Equipe Sports, both in Stratton Village, carry pro bikes and accessories.

Trail identification: Bike trails are indicated by white arrows on an orange circle; hiking trails have white hiker silhouettes on an orange circle.

Special features: Stratton offers a mountain bike package at $43–70 per person, per day, double occupancy. It includes a stay in a condo, a gondola pass, a daily mountain bike tour, free use of the Stratton Sports Center, discounts on bike rentals and repairs, and free child care.

Stratton's Kids Kamp has activities for children ages 6–12, its Little Kids Kamp takes children from 3 to 5 years old, and its Childcare Center takes infants and toddlers (6 weeks to 3 years).

Reservation number: 802-297-3001

Internet address: http://stratton.com/stratton/summer/html/
biking.htm

E-mail address: skistratton@intrawest.com

Hiking: Hikers can use the gondola for a trip to the top, for a
trip to the bottom, or for a round-trip. The Appalachian Trail
and the Long Trail, both off-limits to mountain bikes, are
accessible from the top of the lift. A nice hike (out of bounds
for mountain bikers) is from the gondola to the fire lookout
tower and back.

Other activities: Stratton also features a tennis school, a golf
school, and riding stables. On summer weekends, interna-
tionally known performers entertain under the stars at the
edge of the ski slope. There are many restaurants in the Stratton area, and for the shoppers in the family, nearby Manchester features factory outlets.

Festivals: Each fall Stratton hosts the Stratton Arts Festival.

Campground: Jamaica State Park (802-874-4600), 9 miles east
of Bondville on VT 30, has 57 campsites.

Hostel: The Vagabond Youth Hostel (802-874-4096) is on VT 30
in nearby East Jamaica.

Suggested itinerary

You'll probably want to warm up by taking one of the easiest
descents at Stratton. It offers nice views of the Green Mountains
and the Adirondacks, as well as being a sheltered route on a hot
day. The tables outside the lodge at the Sun Bowl are a great place
for a picnic, and you can access the Sun Bowl cross-country trails
without needing a car by riding:

Stratton Trip 1: I-91 to the Sun Bowl

Distance: *4.94 miles*
Terrain: *Ski-area access roads and trails*

Difficulty: *Moderate*
Time: *50 minutes*
Elevation loss: *1700 feet*

0.00 *After the 11-minute gondola ride, head toward the* MIKE'S WAY *sign, which is just beyond a bike-trail sign.*

Mike's Way is a dirt access road that provides an easy ski or snowboard run in winter. But during the rest of the year, on a mountain bike, it is a steep, rocky descent with views of the Adirondack Mountains of New York State straight ahead.

0.35 *With Mount Bromley off to the left, follow Mike's Way to the right.*

The trail soon becomes a singletrack from which you have a good view of Gale Mountain Pond.

0.87 *Turn right onto a dirt road, a ski trail known as Interstate 91.*

0.96 *You pass under the gondola, ride around the upper tower of the American Express lift, and go by the midmountain restaurant, closed in summer. Then veer left as the trail winds its way around a lift tower. Where the dirt road goes left, you go straight ahead onto a singletrack.*

1.86 *By Grizzly Lift 8, go right following the I-91 sign. This next section is nicely shaded on a hot summer day.*

2.94 *Leave the woods and descend a ski run, which in summer is a beautiful meadow. At the junction with a pond on the left and the Sun Bowl Lodge on the right, go right to the lodge.*

3.12 *After about 30 minutes, you arrive at the Sun Bowl Lodge, which has an emergency phone.*

You can have a picnic on the tables of the deck or ride some of the Sun Bowl cross-country ski trails, which are mountain bike trails in summer.

Continue back to the main lodge by retracing your route to the junction with the pond, where you go right toward the parking lot.

3.21 At the parking lot, go left past rows C, D, E, and F and begin climbing the dirt road with the MOUNTAIN BIKE TRAIL sign.

Note: This trail is very poorly marked in the clockwise direction.

4.41 After a series of turns you arrive at a four-way junction and go left up the steep hill. At the bottom of Craig's Run, descend to the right. Veer left when you see some condos and a view of Dover and the hill beyond Dover to the right. Ride past some lift towers; the main road veers to the right, passing under another lift and veering right toward the Stratton Village clock tower.

4.94 You're back at the main lodge, where you'll find a drinking fountain and rest rooms.

As you head back up the gondola, you're probably ready for a more difficult descent featuring some moderately technical trails, pretty views, and a nice trail past vacation homes:

Stratton Trip 2: Wanderer

Distance: 2.40 miles
Terrain: Ski-area access roads and trails
Difficulty: Moderate
Time: 25 minutes
Elevation loss: 1620 feet

0.00 After taking the 11-minute gondola ride to Stratton's 3859-foot summit, go right toward the UPPER WANDERER sign.

This route varies between a narrow trail and a singletrack. It is very steep and rocky, with numerous switchbacks and water bars.

You leave the woods of Upper Wanderer and turn right onto Mike's Way, a wider dirt trail.

Spring thaws transform Mike's Way from an easy ski run into a challenging descent through a meadow of wildflowers.

Sasha Immler descends a run at Stratton Mountain.

0.61 To the left of an EAST MEADOW/WEST MEADOW sign, you continue on the trail, which descends directly toward Bromley Mountain, the ski resort several miles to the northeast.

0.87 After 10 minutes, go left onto the Lower Wanderer trail, which takes you through a meadow that has a picnic table.

Now you encounter a very steep section that takes you by beautiful private vacation homes and through some sections shaded by the trees.

You turn left onto a dirt work road and then immediately right onto the trail before the paved road.

2.40 You're back at the gondola.

After a lunch in one of Stratton Village's restaurants, you're probably up for a more challenging singletrack trail. This one was cut through the trees solely for mountain biking:

Stratton Trip 3: Singletrack

Note: Stratton's trail map shows this trail beginning at the summit, to the east of the gondola. But at the time of publication, the upper portion of the trail was being held up by an Act 250 permit, Vermont's law to protect the state from overdevelopment.

Distance: *2.39 miles*
Terrain: *Ski-area access roads and trails*
Difficulty: *Moderate*
Time: *25 minutes*
Elevation loss: *1620 feet*

0.00   After the 11-minute gondola ride, head toward the MIKE'S WAY *sign, which is just beyond a bike-trail sign.*

Mike's Way is a dirt access road that provides an easy ski run in winter but is a steep, rocky descent on a mountain bike. Views are of New York State straight ahead.

0.35   With Mount Bromley off to the left, follow Mike's Way to the right.

The trail soon becomes a singletrack from which you have a good view of Gale Mountain Pond.

0.60   Go left into woods opposite the WEST MEADOW/EAST MEADOW *sign.*

This is a difficult, steep descent through a beautiful, very green, almost tropical section with lots of ferns. About halfway through, you can escape to the work road or continue descending the singletrack.

0.86   After 11 minutes you leave the trees, enter a meadow, and turn right onto a work road. After riding under the gondola, go left onto a trail.

1.48   Where the road goes right, you go straight under the gondola onto a trail that becomes a steep singletrack leading you straight onto Ethan's Alley.

2.39   You're back at the gondola.

At the end of the day, you can drive (or take the last gondola and ride) over to the Sun Bowl, Stratton's cross-country area, to explore some trails unknown to most of Stratton's visitors—such as:

Stratton Trip 4: Old North Cemetery

Distance: *1.35 miles*
Terrain: *Cross-country ski trails and access roads*
Difficulty: *Easy*
How to get there: *This ride starts from the Sun Bowl Base Lodge. Continue past the main downhill ski area. At 1.0 mile, turn right at the Sun Bowl sign onto Mountain Road. At 1.4 miles, make another right following the Sun Bowl sign and arrive at the Sun Bowl Base Lodge area at mile 1.7. Trails start to the left (east) of the Sun Bowl Base Lodge by the cross-country ski sign and map.*
Time: *17 minutes*
Elevation gain: *170 feet*

0.00 *Enter the woods via the trail to the left of the large cross-country ski map sign, which is opposite the Sun Bowl Base Lodge.*

A sign on the trail warns of horses on the path and asks the cyclist to stop and get permission from the tour guide before passing them.

You ride through a difficult muddy section and then veer right from the singletrack onto a dirt road at the junction following the TRAILS *1 2 3 4 sign. You soon cross a culvert. At the junction with Trail 2, veer right to stay on Trail 1. Then, at an unsigned junction with Trail 6, go left around what appears to be a field with a split-rail fence.*

0.31 *At the junction with Trail 4, turn right and ride over to the fence.*

What you thought was a field is actually the Old North Cemetery. This spot is the final resting place of one Mary Styles, described on her tombstone as AN AFFECTIONATE WIFE AND MOTHER AND A DEVOTED CHRISTIAN. Also buried here in the early 1800s were members of the Kidder family, early settlers for whom nearby Kidder Brook was named.

Leaving the cemetery, turn to the right onto Trail 4. This is the nearly overgrown singletrack to the right, not the wide gravel road straight ahead.

0.60 *After gaining 50 feet in 7 minutes, you turn left onto a wide gravel road, which is unsigned Trail 1. This takes you back to the Old North Cemetery, where you go right.*

0.71 *Turn right onto signed* TRAIL *3 and begin riding the singletrack. At the top of a steep climb is a hut for cross-country ski races. Go left onto unsigned Trail 2.*

1.12 *At the junction with Trail 1, with the cemetery still visible to your left, go right and cross the culvert again.*

1.21 *With the cupola of the Sun Bowl Base Lodge visible straight ahead, leave the dirt road and go left onto a singletrack.*

1.35 *You're back at the start.*

If you want to explore one more cross-country trail, you may want to consider:

Stratton Trip 5: Kidder Brook

Distance: *2.23 miles*
Terrain: *Cross-country ski area access roads and trails*
Difficulty: *Moderate*
How to get there: *This ride also starts from the Sun Bowl Base Lodge.*
Time: *40 minutes*
Elevation gain: *350 feet*

0.00 *Enter the woods via the trail to the left of the large cross-country ski map sign, which is opposite the Sun Bowl Base Lodge.*

A sign on the trail warns of horses on the path and asks the cyclist to stop and get permission from the tour guide before passing them.

You ride through a difficult muddy section and then veer right from the singletrack onto a dirt road at the junction following the TRAILS 1 2 3 4 sign. You soon cross a culvert. At the junction with Trail 2, veer right to stay on Trail 1. Then, at an unsigned junction with Trail 6, go left around what appears to be a field with a split-rail fence.

0.24 *With the Old North Cemetery straight ahead, go right onto unsigned Trail 6 and descend. Then go straight up a hill over a wooden bridge signed CARRIAGE BRIDGE (or cross the stream by riding through it to the left of the bridge) and continue riding uphill over another plank bridge on the rocky road.*

0.76 *Leave the woods and enter a grassy clearing from which you can hear Kidder Brook. Here you go left, following signed TRAIL 7 and TRAIL 9, and descend on an easy singletrack.*

0.84 *Turn left onto signed TRAIL 7, a delightfully green, partially shaded section thick with ferns. Go through one slippery, rocky section. Where Trail 7 goes directly next to the main trail, veer to the right and downhill, staying on the signed TRAIL 7.*

You parallel an old stone wall, perhaps from the Kidder era, and pass a large mound. Pass through a wet, mucky section and then, with a brook on your right, continue up the hill to the left.

1.50 *After ascending 260 feet in 20 minutes, go left at the top of the hill onto the wide, main Trail 6.*

1.52 *Climb to the right onto signed TRAIL 8, which in places is steep, rocky, and slippery. You go left at the T and then, after a climb through several muddy spots, go right at the signed junction with connector Trail 6.*

1.83 *At the T with a connector trail to Trail 9, go right and descend. You'll encounter a very muddy section, which may be closed in wet weather. Cross a wooden bridge and go left at the T.*

2.23 *You're back at the start.*

7
Killington, Vermont

Killington is one of the largest—if not *the* largest—ski area in the Northeast. It has numerous mountain biking trails, with varied terrain. And although it has bike shops, restaurants, shops, and entertainment in the evening, nothing is centrally located and I never get the feeling that I'm at a "resort."

Although 4241-foot Killington Peak is only Vermont's second highest peak, it is the highest open to mountain bikes. (Mountain bikes are banned from the summit of 4393-foot Mount Mansfield.) Killington's K-I gondola reaches 4195 feet, making it the highest in the state.

It was apparently named after a Killington in Northumberland, England. But in 1800 the name of the town was changed to Sherburne to honor Col. Benjamin Sherburne. Most of the early landowners lived in Connecticut and some of the earliest town records are in the handwriting of Ezra Stiles, a founder of Brown University, the president of Yale from 1778 to 1795, and one of the most educated men in New England at that time.

In 1961, on the 200th anniversary of its founding, the name of the town was changed back to Killington.

One story says that the name "Vermont" was first applied to this area in 1763 from the top of Killington's summit. According to this version, a Rev. Samuel Peters made the ascent and christened the wilderness "Verd-Mont."

Like many other resorts in Vermont during the Depression,

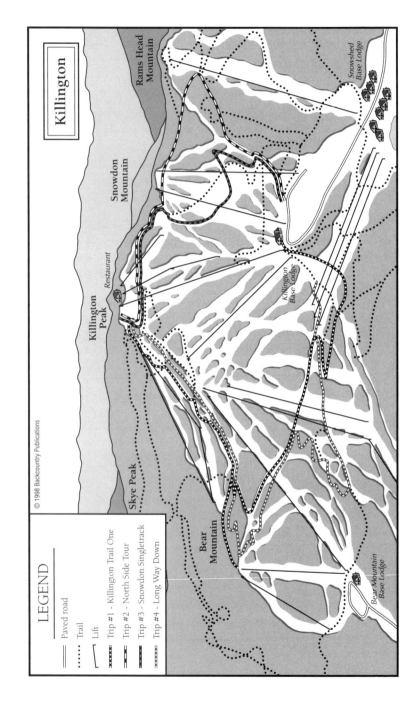

© 1998 Backcountry Publications

LEGEND

Paved road
Trail
Lift
Trip #1 - Killington Trail One
Trip #2 - North Side Tour
Trip #3 - Snowdon Singletrack
Trip #4 - Long Way Down

Killington

Rams Head Mountain

Snowdon Mountain

Killington Peak

Restaurant

Skye Peak

Bear Mountain

Snowshed Base Lodge

Killington Base Lodge

Bear Mountain Base Lodge

Killington had a Civilian Conservation Corps (CCC) camp. CCC crews built some of the roads that today carry vacationers to the slopes.

How to get there: From I-91, take exit 6 and follow VT 103 for 23 miles west to Ludlow. Two miles northwest of Ludlow, take VT 100 for 14 miles north to US 4. Take US 4 west for 4 miles and, following the Killington signs, take Killington Road 5 miles south to the ski area at the top of Killington Road.

From Rutland, take US 4 for 13 miles east and go right (south) on Killington Road 5 miles to the Killington ski area.

Total miles of biking available: 50+

The lift: Of Killington's 15 lifts, only the K-I gondola is open during most of the mountain biking season. Your bike hangs from a rack on the gondola cabin. During foliage season, a second lift, the Skyeship Gondola, which you reach from US 4, runs to the top of 3800-foot Skye Peak.

On the 10-minute ride to the top, as you parallel Roaring Brook you'll see a waterfall and wildflowers of many colors, especially yellow, purple, and white, in spring and summer.

You ride through an upper-transition forest consisting of yellow birch, fire cherry (so called because it thrives in burned areas), sugar maple, quaking aspen, mountain maple, mountain ash or the woodpecker tree (a member of the rose family), and striped maple. At the upper elevations, you enter a boreal forest dominated by balsam fir.

Season and hours: Killington is open daily 9 AM–6 PM from Memorial Day through Columbus Day weekend.

Prices: An all-day gondola ticket to explore Killington's 50 miles of trails costs $25 ($15 juniors). One trip to the top is $20 ($12 juniors); a trail pass is $8 ($5 juniors).

Rental bikes: Bike-rental prices range from $20 for 2 hours on a standard bike to $52 per day for a bike with full suspension.

Helmets and trail passes are included in the bike rental.

Bike shop: The Mountain Bike Shop, open daily 9 AM–6 PM, is a full-service rental, repair, and retail shop.

Trail identification: At Killington the mountain bike trails are marked by a blue sign with a white number, a white arrow, and a mountain bike logo. Hiking trails are marked by white squares with green numbers, arrows, and a hiking logo.

Special features: Killington's trails—50 miles on five mountains—are so extensive that the resort offers guided 2-hour ($60 per person) and 4-hour ($75 per person) tours.

You can have your photo taken at the summit, and you can dine at the Killington Peak Restaurant until 3:30 PM.

If you've brought your children with you, but they're still mastering training wheels, Killington maintains a licensed childcare facility. Call for reservations.

Skiers and boarders complain that many of Killington's trails are not true ski runs, but simply flat, boring connector trails. In summer, though, those same connector trails offer miles of moderate riding alternatives to the steeper singletracks.

And, last but not least, there is a wash stand with 8 hoses so that everyone can clean off their bike at day's end.

Reservation number: 1-800-372-2007

Internet address: http://www.killington.com/summer/biking.html

E-mail address: info@killington.com

Hiking: Killington features the Merrell Hiking Center, the starting point for more than 45 miles of trails. A trail map and pocket field guide are $5. For $10 you get the map, the pocket field guide, and a chairlift ride. The center will even rent you a pair of Merrell hiking boots.

Daily tours 10 AM–12:30 PM and 1:30–4 PM are $14 for adults and $8 for children.

Weekend Hiking Adventures, including daily gondola

passes and 2 nights' lodging, are available for $56 per person, double occupancy.

Other activities: The Ski-Bike-Run triathalon is held Memorial Day weekend. In addition, the area holds 2 NORBA-sanctioned races during the season: Trail 66 and Thunder and Lightning. Killington also features golf, the Killington School for Tennis, and Symphonies Under the Stars. The Killington Stage Race, a road-biking event, is held each summer. Many establishments in the Killington area offer dining and evening entertainment.

Although Pico (9 miles to the east on US 4), recently purchased by the American Skiing Company—owners of Killington—no longer offers mountain biking, it still features an alpine slide, miniature golf, a driving range, and "the bungee thing."

When Killington acquired Pico, they made a deal with the Forest Service. Killington gave up mountain bike access on the south side, the Juggernaut and Solitude trails, and in return is developing mountain bike trails that will connect Killington with Pico.

Campgrounds: Close by (1 mile north on VT 100), Gifford Woods State Park (802-775-5354) has 48 campsites. Coolidge State Park (802-672-3612) at nearby Plymouth (4 miles east on US 4, 5 miles south on VT 100, then 5 miles east on VT 100A), the birthplace of President Coolidge, has 60 campsites. The Sugar House Campground (802-672-5043) in Plymouth (4 miles east on US 4, then 5 miles south on VT 100) has 45 campsites.

Hostel: At the Trojan Horse Hostel (44 Andover Street; 802-228-5244 or 1-800-547-7475; e-mail: thlodge@aol.com), just south of Ludlow on VT 100, you can stay in an old carriage barn. Ludlow is about 25 miles south of Killington on scenic Route 103.

Suggested itinerary

Killington's gondola takes you to within 46 feet of the actual summit. It can't be reached by mountain bike, but you may want to take the 10–15 minutes to reach it via the self-guided nature trail:

Killington Peak

Terrain: *Hiking trail*
Difficulty: *Easy*
Time: *12 minutes*
Elevation gain: *46 feet*

0.00   *Immediately after you exit the gondola, leave your bike and proceed to the right onto Hiking Trail 1; then go left at Sign 1A.*

As you climb along the self-guided nature trail, there are signs identifying wood sorrel, balsam fir, starflower, mountain ash, skunk currant, heart-leaved white birch, and the pin (or fire) cherry. Each sign shows the plant's leaf. In about 6 minutes you've reached the actual 4241-foot summit of Killington. The fire tower would give you an even better view, but it is usually closed to the public.

Continue on the trail in a clockwise direction, and in about 12 minutes, you're back at the gondola.

Now you're ready for a long trip that offers easy roads, single-tracks, and views from the top of Bear Mountain:

Killington Trip 1: Killington Trail One

Distance: *6.10 miles*
Terrain: *Ski-area access roads and trails*
Difficulty: *Moderate*
Time: *1 hour*

Elevation loss: *1870 feet*
Elevation gain: *150 feet*

0.00 Leave the gondola and follow the TRAIL 1 sign down a moderately steep, rocky descent that curves to the left. At the junction
of Trails 1, 2, and 7, veer right onto Trail 1, the signed JUGGER-
NAUT ski trail.

This is a combination of work road and pleasant, easy singletrack.

2.79 After dropping 1000 feet in 30 minutes, pass the junction with
Trail 6 and continue to follow Trail 1. You then go right onto a
dirt road—the Frostline ski run—and descend.

2.95 At the junction with a wooden power pole, leave Trail 1 and turn
right past a six-sided building (it has an emergency phone.)

From the top of the Bear Mountain ski area, you have a view
that includes 3150-foot Mount Ascutney, the highest and
most prominent peak to the west. Far off to the left is New
Hampshire's Presidential Range, topped by 6288-foot Mount
Washington.

*Back at the power pole, keep straight on Trail 1 and descend
the gravel road.*

4.29 Leave the road and go right following the TRAIL 1 sign toward
the lift tower.

4.89 Turn left onto the gravel road and climb up to a small summit,
from which you have an excellent view of the Snowshed Base
Lodge area. Then just before the paved road, veer left on a dirt
road toward the main Killington Base Lodge.

5.50 You're back at the Killington Base Lodge and the Mountain Bike
Center.

After a break, perhaps you're ready to explore the northern side
of the mountain via a moderate ride on a rough gravel road with
a nice stretch on a singletrack and views of the main resort area:

Killington Trip 2: North Side Tour

Distance: *3.16 miles*
Terrain: *Ski-area access roads and trails*
Difficulty: *Moderate*
Time: *30 minutes*
Elevation loss: *1630 feet*
Elevation gain: *100 feet*

0.00   *You leave the gondola and follow the* TRAIL 1 *sign down a moderately steep, rocky descent that curves to the left.*

0.12   *At the junction of Trail 1 and Trail 2, go straight on Trail 7, veer slightly to the left, then veer right at the* TRAIL 7 *sign just below the Killington Peak Restaurant onto the signed* GREAT EASTERN *ski run, which goes underneath the K-1 gondola.*

Several TRAIL 7 signs have arrows that make it appear that the trail goes left, but you should just continue straight on the gravel road.

1.39   *To get a break from the rough gravel road, just before the Snowdon Triple lift leave the gravel road, which is Trail 7, and go right onto a singletrack signed* TRAIL 7 (SINGLETRACK). *This descends through a meadow, enters the woods, and becomes a technical singletrack. Leave the singletrack and go right onto the gravel road. This is unsigned Trail 7, a very pleasant downhill section.*

3.16   *You're back at the Mountain Bike Center.*

Now you can have lunch on the deck of the lodge. Or you can get back on the gondola and have lunch at the Killington Peak Restaurant, which has wonderful views of the Green Mountains. After lunch you can warm up by doing:

Killington Trip 3: Snowdon Singletrack

Distance: *3.05 miles*
Terrain: *Ski-area access roads and trails*

Difficulty: *Moderate*
Time: *30 minutes*
Elevation loss: *1620 feet*

0.00   You leave the gondola and follow the TRAIL 1 *sign down a moderately steep, rocky descent that curves to the left.*

0.12   At the junction with Trail 1 and Trail 2, go straight on Trail 7, which veers slightly to the left, then to the right at the TRAIL 7 *sign just below the Killington Peak restaurant onto the signed* GREAT EASTERN *ski run.*

0.48   At the top of the South Ridge Triple chairlift, veer left and follow the TRAIL 7 *sign.*

0.63   Ride underneath the K-I gondola.

Several TRAIL 7 signs have arrows that make it appear that the trail goes left, but you should just continue straight on the gravel road.

1.27   At the T, where Trail 7 climbs to the left, take in the view of the main ski runs, then go right onto Trail 21.

1.35   After 10 minutes you veer left and enter the woods onto a singletrack that provides terrific views as you traverse the Royal Flush and High Line ski trails, from which you get nice views of the base area. Go right onto Trail 20, then immediately left onto Trail 21, a descending singletrack. Leave the woods and turn left onto a road, which is Trail 7.

3.05   You're back at the Mountain Bike Center.

Now you're ready for one last, long run of the day:

Killington Trip 4: The Great Eastern

Distance: *4.75 miles*
Terrain: *Ski-area access roads and trails*
Difficulty: *Moderate*
Time: *1 hour*

Elevation loss: 1550 feet
Elevation gain: 430 feet

0.00 Leave the gondola and follow the TRAIL 1 sign down a moderately steep, rocky descent that curves to the left. At the junction of Trails 1, 2, and 7, go straight on Trail 7, which veers slightly to the left.

At the TRAIL 7 sign just below The Killington Peak restaurant, veer right onto the signed GREAT EASTERN ski run.

Veer right onto Trail 26, the GREAT EASTERN. This becomes Trail 1.

1.75 After 30 minutes, you exit the woods. At a T, go right onto Trail 6 and descend.

2.49 Turn right onto the dirt road, which is Trail 1. Then, at the GREAT EASTERN sign, go right onto Trail 6 and descend.

3.45 Turn left onto the work road. This is Trail 2, which soon veers to the left up the hill.

3.99 At the junction, veer left up the hill onto Trail 1 and continue straight past the junction with Trail 24. At the Snowshed lift, ride straight across the plateau. At the junction where Trail 1 goes uphill to the left, go straight across the unsigned dirt road onto Trail 25, an easy singletrack that descends through the woods. Exit the woods and, with the main lodge straight ahead, veer to the right following Trail 25. Leave the singletrack and go left onto an unsigned work road.

4.75 You're back at the Mountain Bike Center.

8

Sugarbush, Vermont

Sugarbush is in the Green Mountains' beautiful Mad River Valley, named because of the river's frenzied run down the hills. Maybe it's because it's a little bit of a drive from the interstate, but Sugarbush has never really developed into the more glitzy type of resort like Killington. It resembles more the smaller, low-key resorts that do not open their lifts in the summer—but it does have lift-accessed mountain biking.

Sugarbush is in the town of Warren, which was probably named for Dr. Joseph Warren, an early patriot killed in the battle of Bunker Hill during the Revolutionary War. Sugarbush South's highest point, 2400-foot Lincoln Peak, was not named for President Lincoln but after the nearby town of Lincoln. However, 2237-foot Nancy Hanks Peak honors Lincoln's mother. Sugarbush North's 2650-foot Mount Ellen was named for Ellen Douglas, Sir Walter Scott's "Lady of the Lake," by young people working on the Long Trail.

How to get there: From I-89 southbound, take exit 10 to US 2 east to VT 100 south, to the Sugarbush Access Road. From I-91, take I-89 north to exit 9, Middlesex. Go east on US 2 to VT 100B to VT 100 south, to the Sugarbush Access Road. Go right (west) on the Sugarbush Access Road to the Lincoln Peak area (not Mt. Ellen). It's about 18 miles from either interstate exit to Sugarbush.

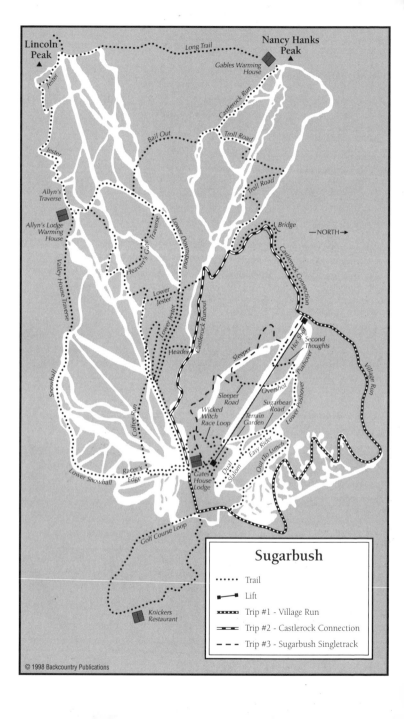

Lincoln Peak ▲

Long Trail

Nancy Hanks Peak ▲

Gables Warming House

Jester

Castlerock Run

Troll Road

Bail Out

Troll Road

Jester

← NORTH →

Allyn's Traverse

Bridge

Allyn's Lodge Warming House

Castlerock Connection

Lower Downhill

Heaven's Gate

Valley House Traverse

Lower Jester

Hot Shot

Sleeper

Second Thoughts

Lower Jester

Castlerock Runout

Village Run

Header

Overshot

Pushover

Snowball

Sleeper Road

Lower Pushover

Coffee Run

Wicked Witch Race Loop

Sugarbear Road

Terrain Garden

Easy Rider

Out To Lunch

Racer's Edge

Gates House Lodge

Dual Slalom

Lower Snowball

Golf Course Loop

Knickers Restaurant

Sugarbush

· · · · · · Trail

■━● Lift

▨▨▨▨ Trip #1 - Village Run

▤▤▤▤ Trip #2 - Castlerock Connection

– – – – Trip #3 - Sugarbush Singletrack

© 1998 Backcountry Publications

Total miles of biking available: 40+

The lift: After paying for your lift ticket, you are required to watch a 5-minute video on mountain biking safety. Then you'll ride up the mountain on a detachable quad chairlift. (Your bike rides up on a different chair.) The slope under the quad is barren, but you ride through stands of birch, ash, and, especially, the maples for which Sugarbush is named. Although hikers have access to the entire mountain, the Forest Service restricts cyclists to the lower mountain. Be sure to turn around during the 8-minute ride to take in the beautiful views of the Mad River Valley.

Season and hours: Sugarbush is open from late June through Columbus Day weekend. Trails are open daily 8 AM–5 PM. Lift-accessed mountain biking is available Friday through Sunday and holidays 9 AM–4 PM.

Prices: An all-day pass is $22; a single chairlift ride is $8; a trail pass costs $8.

Rental bikes: A full-suspension bike rents for $35 all day, $25 for a half-day.

Bike shop: Sugarbush has a full-service bike shop.

Trail identification: Trails are signed with white numbers on blue squares. Directions are indicated by black arrows. Sugarbush trails also feature the NORBA-recommended symbols for warning cyclists of trail conditions. A single red vertical arrow indicates caution. Double red vertical arrows call for extra caution. Triple red vertical arrows indicate extreme caution.

Special features: Camp Sugarbush is available for youngsters ages 6–12.

Reservation number: 1-800-53-SUGAR

Internet address: http://www.sugarbush.com/sugarbush/sugarbush.shtml

E-mail address: info@sugarbush.com

Hiking: Sugarbush features the Dolomite Trekking Center. A single chairlift ride is $8. You can hike to 3975-foot Lincoln Peak on a section of the Long Trail. Six-hour guided treks for groups of four or more are $20. Because the Forest Service restricts mountain bikers to the lower mountain, the upper mountain is essentially the hiker's private domain.

Other activities: Sugarbush also has golf, soaring, horseback riding, fly-fishing, canoeing, theater, Vermont Symphony Orchestra concerts, polo, horse shows, tennis, and personalized fitness training. Many Mad River Valley establishments, such as Warren's The Common Man, offer nightly dining.

Festivals: Typical activities and festivals include the Strawberry Jubilee; Ben & Jerry's One World, One Heart Festival; New England Regional Soaring Championships; the Sugarbush Cricket Festival; the Mad River Valley Road Bike Race; arts festivals; and the Sugarbush Brewers Festival.

Campground: The closest campground, Gifford Woods State Park (802-775-5354), 37 miles to the south on VT 100, has 48 campsites.

Suggested itinerary

For your first run down the hill, you'll probably want to try an easy dirt road with a moderate singletrack and an easy paved return:

Sugarbush Trip 1: Village Run

Distance: 2.65 miles
Terrain: Ski-area access roads, trails, and paved roads
Difficulty: Moderate
Time: 20 minutes
Elevation loss: 930 feet

0.00 You leave the lift and head right, toward the Slide Brook

Sugarbush, Vermont

Express lift, and bear right following the TRAIL #6 *sign.*

Entering the shelter of the numerous sugar maple trees, you'll encounter the first of several stream crossings. Usually water bars are dry, but one brook actually crosses in one.

0.73 *After descending 200 feet in 7 minutes, you leave the road and enter the woods on a singletrack, steep in places, whose edges are outlined by small logs. The trees on the boundaries of the singletrack are also blazed with blue tape. After leaving the singletrack, go right onto a wide dirt road that winds past many resort homes until it becomes paved Village Drive.*

1.97 *Go right on paved Summit Drive, which passes a fire station with an enormous number of mailboxes. Opposite a* LINCOLN PEAK PARKING *sign, you turn right into the Sugarbush parking lot.*

2.65 *You're back at the lift.*

You've explored the northern side of Sugarbush; now you're ready for the southern side, a moderate descent on dirt roads with views of the Mad River Valley, several stream crossings, and views of waterfalls:

Sugarbush Trip 2: Castlerock Connection

Distance: *1.78 miles*
Terrain: *Ski-area access roads and trails*
Difficulty: *Moderate*
Time: *15 minutes*
Elevation loss: *840 feet*

0.00 *You leave the lift and head left toward the North Lynx chairlift. Just beyond the lift, go left onto the Castlerock Connection Trail.*

This trail crosses numerous water bars and goes past maples and some really huge birch trees. Twice—either on a small wooden bridge or over a water bar—you cross the Clay Brook, which has pretty falls on the right.

0.84 *Having lost 370 feet in 7 minutes, you encounter a sharp, sweeping turn to the left as you pass the junction of Trails #5 and #7. You continue to the left on Trail #7, pass under another lift, and encounter a steep rocky section.*

Clay Brook then crosses under the trail again and flows on the left side.

1.78 *After riding through the resort village, you're back at the lift.*

The resort's restaurant is not open in summer, but the Little Market and Deli, 1/2 mile below the resort, is a great place to buy snacks or sandwiches.

Primarily you've been descending on roads—you're probably ready now for a beautiful ride on tree-lined trails and moderately technical singletracks:

Sugarbush Trip 3: Sugarbush Singletrack

Distance: *1.32 miles*
Terrain: *Ski-area access roads and trails*

Difficulty: *Moderate*
Time: *12 minutes*
Elevation loss: *810 feet*

0.00 *After you leave the lift, immediately go left and descend, paralleling the lift line. Where Trail #9 goes straight, you veer right onto Trail #10, Sleeper.*

You'll pass through a meadow with occasional birch trees alongside the trail. Trail #10 veers to the right and enters the woods.

0.90 *After a drop of 690 feet in 6 minutes, you now ride a singletrack on which potentially dangerous stumps have been painted orange. You exit the woods, go right, and descend under the quad.*

1.32 *You're back at the lift.*

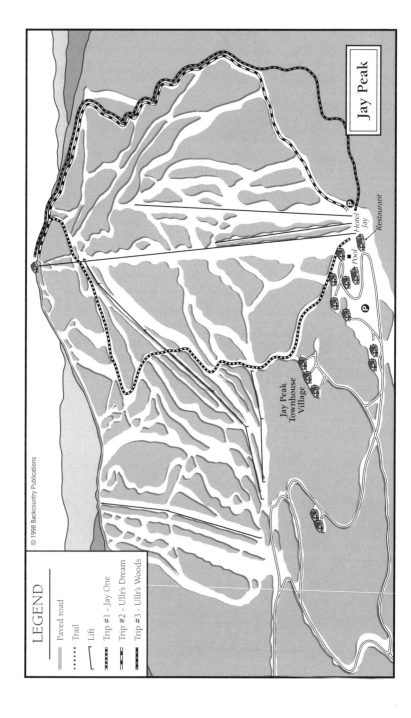

LEGEND

Paved road
Trail
Lift
Trip #1 - Jay One
Trip #2 - Ullr's Dream
Trip #3 - Ullr's Woods

© 1998 Backcountry Publications

Jay Peak

Jay Peak
Townhouse
Village

Hotel
Jay

Restaurant

Pool

9
Jay Peak, Vermont

Jay is about as far north as you can get in Vermont without going into Canada. If you're looking for a low-key resort at a mountain that offers unique and superb views—and a nice mix of downhill and singletrack trails—try Jay Peak.

The town of Jay and 3870-foot Jay Peak both were named after John Jay (1745–1829), one of the nation's founding fathers, the first chief justice of the United States Supreme Court, and a two-term governor of New York State.

"But isn't this Vermont?" you ask. Why commemorate a New Yorker? The town and peak were named after him and Jay was given 15,600 acres in this region for his help in settling a land dispute between the two states.

Some of the original trails were built by a Civilian Conservation Corps crew during the Depression, but the ski resort in its current form was built by the Weyerhaeuser Corporation. Its influence can be seen in the amount of wood used in the tram stations. In 1979 Weyerhaeuser sold the resort to a Canadian company, Mount Saint Saveur, that operates eight ski areas: Jay Peak, six resorts in Canada, and one in France. As this book went to press, plans were underway to sell the resort to another Canadian company, Lifestyle Resorts International of Barrie, Ontario.

Mount Mansfield and Killington are higher, but perhaps because of its Fuji-like shape, or maybe because you can see

Montréal, at Jay you feel you're on the top of the world. Jay can also have top-of-the-world-like weather. On one fall day, there was even ice on the top.

How to get there: From the United States, take I-91 to exit 26. Follow signs to Jay Peak; this takes you north on US 5, then north on VT 14, southwest on VT 100, north on VT 101, and west on VT 242 to Jay Peak.

From Canada, take Autoroute 10 to exit 106 and follow signs to Jay Peak.

Total miles of biking available: 20

The lift: Jay Peak has the only tram in Vermont. A nice thing about the tram is its capacity. Once my bike and I shared it with two hikers, their backpacks, and a class of elementary school students. Even with all those people and their equipment, the 60-passenger tram still didn't feel crowded.

The tram leaves every 30 minutes. An attendant accompanies you, pointing out the peak to the east known as Owl's Head; 32-mile-long Lake Memphremagog, which spans the Canadian border (just 6 miles to the north); the skyline of Montréal (visible on a clear day); 4393-foot Mount Mansfield (the highest point in Vermont); and 6288-foot Mount Washington (the highest point in New England). From the upper tram station, which has rest room facilities, it's about a 50-foot climb up some wooden steps to the actual summit of Jay Peak. The tram doesn't operate in extremely windy conditions.

You can clean off your bike with a hose at the entrance to the lower tram station.

Season and hours: Jay is open daily from late June through Labor Day and then weekends until Columbus Day.

Prices: An all-day lift ticket, including use of the swimming pool, is $18. Two rides up on the tram are $15; one ride is $10. A trail pass is $5.

Rental bikes: Jay Peak has no rental bikes, but bikes can be rented in Newport at the Great Outdoors Trading Company, 73 Main Street, 802-334-2831.

Bike shop: There is no bike shop, but the ski shop has some tools in the summer.

Trail identification: Trails are identified by downhill ski and cross-country ski trail signs.

Reservation numbers: 802-988-2611; 1-800-451-4449

Internet address: http://jaypeakresort.com/jay-peak/html/summer.htm

E-mail address: JayPeak@together.net

Hiking: The Long Trail crosses Jay Peak.

Other activities: A crafts fair is held each Columbus Day weekend, and there's a Triple Crank race series throughout the summer.

Campground: The Millbrook Campground (802-744-6673) in Westfield (10 miles from Jay Peak at the junction of VT 100 and VT 101) has 30 campsites.

Suggested itinerary

Start off with a tour of Jay's southern side via a steep dirt road, some trails, and singletracks:

Jay Trip 1: Jay One

Distance: 2.72 miles
Terrain: Ski-area access roads and trails
Difficulty: Moderate
Time: 25 minutes
Elevation loss: 2040 feet

0.00 *After getting off the tram and leaving the tram building, go left onto the Northway trail, which makes a sharp turn to the right signed* EASIER WAY.

Cyclists descend beneath the tram at Jay Peak.

By a large trail map sign, Northway veers to the right and becomes a steep, rocky descent that uses plywood sheets as bridges to cross the numerous water bars.

1.20 At the orange nylon catch fence, after 12 minutes and 1040 feet of descending, go left onto Angel's Wiggle 11, which parallels a brook, crosses it, and then becomes a singletrack through a meadow.

1.53 You cross a small wooden bridge and then begin a slight climb to the left onto Taxi 19, which is a singletrack that is at first muddy and then becomes a short but rocky technical section.

1.79 Where Can Am and Taxi go right, you keep riding straight onto a singletrack into the woods. Then, when you exit the woods, go right onto an unmarked ski run.

1.99 You go left onto signed QUEENS HIGHWAY 17 following the RAM/ BASE AREA sign. By a house on the right, the trail veers to the left, then directly under the tram. Head right toward the base area.

2.72 You're back at the start.

Next you descend the northern side of Jay on:

Jay Trip 2: Ullr's Dream

Distance: *2.76 miles*
Terrain: *Ski-area access roads and trails*
Difficulty: *Moderate*
Time: *25 minutes*
Elevation loss: *2020 feet*

0.00   After getting off the tram and leaving the tram building, go left onto the Northway trail, which makes a sharp turn to the right signed EASIER WAY.

0.35   Turn left onto Ullr's Dream 30, named after Ullr, the Norse god of snow.

0.73   With a pond straight ahead, the trail veers to the left of the wooden snow fence.

0.85   After an extremely steep and rocky descent, go right following the TRAM/BASE AREA sign.

1.23   After dropping 1180 feet in 13 minutes, you ride down an incredibly steep area over several water bars covered with sheets of plywood, and veer left at the bottom of the JFK ski run.

1.79   At the junction with the Upper Ullr's cross-country trail entrance, keep riding straight as you pass under a chairlift.

2.58   After an easy run between the trees, you veer right, climb slightly, then go left toward the tram building.

2.76   You're at the tram building once again.

After a lunch at the restaurant, you're probably ready to do some singletrack, such as:

Jay Trip 3: Ullr's Woods

Distance: *3.11 miles*

Terrain: *Ski-area access roads and trails*
Difficulty: *Moderate*
Time: *45 minutes*
Elevation loss: *2010 feet*

0.00 *After getting off the tram and leaving the tram building, go left onto the Northway trail, which makes a sharp turn to the right signed EASIER WAY.*

0.35 *Turn left onto Ullr's Dream 30, which veers to the left of a wooden snow fence, by a pond.*

0.85 *After an extremely steep and rocky descent, go right following the TRAM/BASE AREA sign. You ride down an incredibly steep area over several water bars covered with sheets of plywood, and veer left at the bottom of the JFK ski run.*

1.79 *Go left at the junction signed UPPER ULLR'S XC TRAIL ENTRANCE. After a lovely section of trail, just slightly wider than a single-track, veer left at the sign ULLR'S WOODS.*

Cross a brook on a wooden bridge, or ride through the streambed on the left side when the water is low enough. At one point you actually ride through the brook for about 20 yards. Then you cross a stream on a pole-and-plywood bridge and veer left.

2.97 *Turn left at the junction with an ULLR'S WOODS sign and encounter another section where the trail goes through the middle of a streambed for a short distance.*

3.11 *You emerge from the woods and then veer left by a mainte-nance building.*

3.11 *You're back at the tram building.*

On a hot day, this is a good time to take advantage of the pool.

10
Loon Mountain, New Hampshire

Loon, like nearby Franconia Notch, is a place of contrasts. It features what everyone would agree is superb natural beauty but also what some would say is overcommercialization. If you enjoy the commercial attractions, then you'll be happy. If they're not appealing to you, then get on a mountain bike and in a few minutes be hundreds of feet below them.

Loon Mountain is named after the aquatic bird because of a story that loons used to nest in Big Loon Pond, the reservoir for Lincoln, New Hampshire.

Lincoln had been a tourist attraction as early as 1802, when Jeremiah Stuart received a one-year license to operate a public inn and tavern out of his home. But tourists didn't really start arriving in large numbers to see the wonders of Franconia Notch until the 1840s, when railroad travel made it easier to reach.

In the 1890s, Lincoln became a booming mill town, turning the abundant supply of trees into paper products. At the same time, area rooming houses gave way to large hotels.

In 1923, Sherman Adams, a Dartmouth graduate, was in charge of a local mill. Adams later entered politics and became the governor of New Hampshire and President Eisenhower's chief adviser. But during Ike's second term, Adams was forced to resign for accepting gifts from a textile company.

Just as he left office, the paper industry in Lincoln began its decline. As a young man Adams had been a member of the

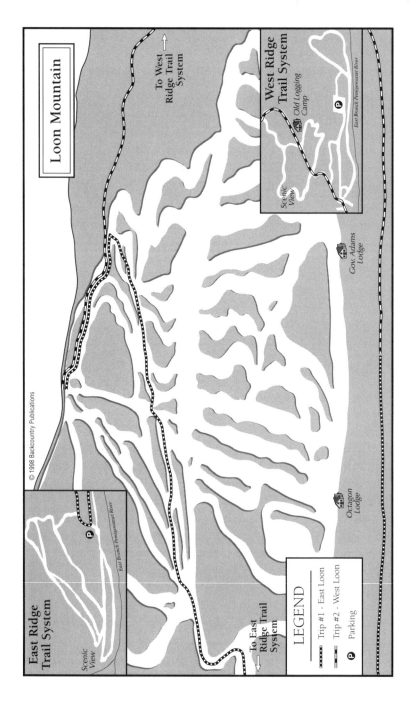

Loon Mountain

© 1998 Backcountry Publications

East Ridge
Trail System

Scenic View

East Branch Pemigewasset River

To East
Ridge Trail
System

West Ridge
Trail System

Scenic
View

Old Logging
Camp

East Branch Pemigewasset River

To West
Ridge Trail
System

Gov. Adams
Lodge

Octagon
Lodge

LEGEND

Trip #1 - East Loon
Trip #2 - West Loon
Parking

Dartmouth Outing Club and knew the White Mountains well. He realized that Loon Mountain would be an excellent location for a ski resort and that it would be easily accessible via the soon-to-be-completed interstate.

Under Sherman Adams's leadership, Loon Mountain began welcoming skiers in December 1966; 25 years later it opened its arms to mountain bikers. Today the observatory on top of Mount Washington is named in Sherman Adams's honor.

How to get there: Take I-93 to exit 32, then go east 4 miles on NH 112, the Kancamagus Highway.

Total miles of biking available: 30.70 miles at the mountain plus the 14.54-mile Franconia Notch trip.

The lift: During most of the season, you ride up in a modern, four-passenger gondola. The doors have window vents and there's another vent on the top, so it's comfortable even on a hot summer day. Your bike rides up on the platform of a separate work car. The 11-minute ride to the top offers views of 3294-foot Big Coolidge, 4328-foot Mount Flume, and 3568-foot Whaleback Mountain.

You can't ride through any part of the summit area and must leave your bike in a rack by the lift tower. So if you want to do any extensive explorations at the top, a bike lock is a good idea. Although hikers can take the last gondola down at 7:15 PM, cyclists are not allowed up after 4 PM.

Note: During July and August, cyclists must take the Kanc Quad to the summit instead of the gondola.

Season: Loon is open late June through Columbus Day weekend, 9 AM–4 PM.

Prices: A full-day lift ticket for an adult is $18 ($15 for juniors), a half-day costs $12 ($10 for juniors), a single ride is $10 ($8 for juniors).

Rental bikes: The Mountain Bike Center rents regular bikes

Rob O'Malley and Tom Hyland ride down Loon Mountain.

for $30 per day, $25 for 4 hours, or $20 for 2 hours. High performance bikes are $35 per day, $30 for 4 hours, or $18 for 2 hours. With lift service it's $45 per day, $30 for 4 hours, or $26 for 2 hours.

Bike shop: The Mountain Bike Center sells and services mountain bikes.

Special features: A Surf and Turf pass, which includes an all-day gondola pass at Loon plus an all-day pass for the nearby Whale's Tale waterpark, is $25.

Reservation number: 603-745-8111, ext. 5400

Internet address: http://www.loonmtn.com/summer/1998/mtbike.html

E-mail address: info@loonmtn.com

Hiking: Hikers can take the gondola up and explore Loon Mountain. Or they can take to the many trails in the Franconia Notch region.

Other activities: You'll find in-line skating, skateboarding, canoeing, hiking, the Mountain Man shows, and the Loon Wildlife Theater. Then there's the lecture series, Tuesdays at 7 PM throughout the summer. Nearby Lincoln features dining and legitimate theater in the evening.

Festivals: A typical summer might include an Americanfest, an Irishfest, a Brewfest, a Cajunfest, the Samuel Adams Professional Lumberjack Festival, and the Bavarian Fall Festival. In mid-September, the town of Lincoln puts on the Highland Games, featuring Scottish athletic games, country dancing, pipe bands, and competitions.

Campgrounds: There are three campgrounds in nearby Woodstock, 4 miles west on NH 112: Maple Haven Camping (603-745-3350) has 39 sites; Broken Branch KOA (603-745-8008) has 130 sites; and Franconia Notch State Park has 98 sites.

Suggested itinerary

At the summit, leave your bike by the gondola and walk to the top of the four-story lookout tower. There you can see 3294-foot Big Coolidge, 4328-foot Mount Flume, and 3568-foot Owl's Head. On a clear day you can also see 5715-foot Mount Jefferson, 5798-foot Mount Adams, and 6288-foot Mount Washington.

Now you're ready to explore the east side of Loon, the shorter, easier way to the bottom:

Loon Trip 1: East Loon Mountain

Distance: *3.52 miles*
Terrain: *Ski-area access roads and trails*
Difficulty: *Moderate*
Map: *Loon*
Time: *30 minutes*
Elevation loss: *1850 feet*
Elevation gain: *110 feet*

0.00 *Leave the gondola tower and immediately descend steeply to the right on the signed bike trail, pass under the gondola, and then immediately turn left under the gondola to an easier singletrack. Then you veer right onto a gravel road, which has numerous water bars.*

0.37 *Veer right from the gravel road onto a dirt road with the ski trail signs* U. PICKED ROCK *and* U. FLYING FOX. *Next you ride—or jump—over some snowmaking pipes on a dirt ramp and then enter a muddy singletrack section before again turning right onto the gravel road. You parallel the gondola for a while, climb for a short distance, and turn right onto a singletrack. Then turn left at the junction in front of a chairlift.*

1.47 *After paralleling the lift line, go right and climb onto a singletrack. You cross a small brook, descend again toward another lift line, then ride through a nice section of singletrack with a stream to the right. Go right onto the gravel road again.*

1.85 *After gaining speed on the road, take the steep trail to the right, which has many muddy water bars and some muddy areas covered by wooden boardwalks, and climb to the right through aspens.*

After another climb, you go left onto a wide trail where there is a X-COUNTRY TRAILS *sign. This is a part of the East Ridge cross-country trail system. You descend, go around a gate, and go left onto an unsigned, paved road. At the stop sign, go right onto another paved road and encounter a fast, paved descent. By the condo with the tennis courts, you veer right and parallel the rocky East Branch of the Pemigewasset River.*

3.52 *You reach the start again.*

After a snack at the mountaintop restaurant, you're ready to try something a little harder and longer:

Loon Trip 2: West Loon

Distance: *5.01 miles*
Terrain: *Ski-area access roads and trails*
Difficulty: *Difficult*
Map: *Loon*
Time: *1 hour*
Elevation loss: *1840 feet*
Elevation gain: *160 feet*

0.00   *Leave the gondola tower and immediately descend steeply to the right on the signed bike trail, pass under the gondola, and then immediately turn left under the gondola to an easier singletrack. Then you veer right onto a gravel road, which has numerous water bars.*

0.37   *Veer right from the gravel road onto a dirt road with the ski trail signs U. PICKED ROCK and U. FLYING FOX. Next you ride, or jump, over some snowmaking pipes on a dirt ramp, and then enter a muddy singletrack section*

0.49   *You cross the road and continue on the muddy singletrack into the woods, which steeply descends over both smooth granite surfaces and loose rocks.*

0.83   *You reach the beautiful Big Loon Pond, a dam supplying water primarily for snowmaking, but also for the town of Lincoln. Follow the trail by riding carefully across the dam.*

After a very muddy section, you encounter a steep climb, which for me was a pusher. After gaining 80 feet, you ride through a very rough section and another muddy section.

3.01   *At the junction with a wider trail, you veer left and ride over a brook.*

Now you're riding a section of the West Ridge cross-country trail system. You reach the site of an old logging camp.

Here, at the junction with Tote Road, you veer right. While at the immediate junction with the Short N Sassy trail, you stay

> straight past the junction signed X-COUNTRY TRAILS into the woods of birch and maple. Go around the gate by a condo and onto a paved road.

4.36 At this junction, there's a dirt road straight ahead that looks tempting. But it's off-limits to mountain bikes, so you go left and descend on the paved road. At the T, turn right onto another unsigned paved road.

5.01 You're at the gondola again.

Although it's entirely paved, you shouldn't miss one of Loon's specialties:

Loon Trip 3: Franconia Notch

The Loon Mountain Park Bike Tour through Franconia Notch is a wonderful way to visit many of the area's most scenic and historic locations.

The Loon shuttle bus leaves four times a day and escorts you to the start of the Franconia Notch Bike Path. It's all downhill from there, and a self-guided brochure available at the Mountain Bike Center leads you the rest of the way through a most memorable biking experience.

Some of the places and attractions along the way include: Echo Lake, Artists Bluff, Cannon Mountain, the New England Ski Museum, the Old Man of the Mountain, Profile Lake, the Basin, Flume Gorge, the Whale's Tale Water Park, and Clark's Trading Post.

Distance: *14.54 miles*
Terrain: *Paved recreational path and paved road*
Difficulty: *Easy to moderate*
Map: *Franconia Notch*
Time: *1 1/3 hours of riding time. Allow 2–3 hours to explore Franconia Notch.*
Elevation loss: *1320 feet*

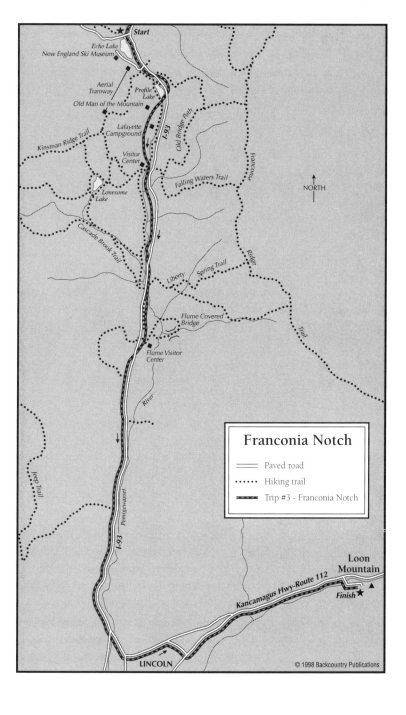

Franconia Notch

═══ Paved road

••••• Hiking trail

▪▪▪▪ Trip #3 - Franconia Notch

★ Start
Echo Lake
New England Ski Museum
Aerial Tramway
Profile Lake
Old Man of the Mountain
Lafayette Campground
Visitor Center
Kinsman Ridge Trail
I-93
Old Bridge Path
Falling Waters Trail
Franconia
NORTH
Lonesome Lake
Cascade Brook Trail
Liberty Spring Trail
Ridge
Flume Covered Bridge
Flume Visitor Center
Trail
River
Pemigewasset
Jeep Trail
I-93
Loon Mountain
Kancamagus Hwy-Route 112
Finish ★
LINCOLN

© 1998 Backcountry Publications

Cost: *The bus trip costs $15 ($10 for juniors). The bus trip plus a 4-hour bike rental is $26 ($21 for juniors).*

0.00　*Right where the bus lets you out is the trailhead for the 30-minute round-trip hike to Artists Bluff, where you can see Echo Lake, lower Cannon Mountain, and parts of Franconia Notch. Cross the road and enter the Recreational Trail. You ride by Echo Lake with Cannon Mountain and the Cannon Mountain Tramway in the background. The 4107-foot peak was called Cannon because a horizontal stone on the summit resembles that weapon.*

0.60　*At the trail junction, go right toward Cannon Mountain.*

0.71　*In the northwest corner of the parking lot for the Cannon Mountain Tramway is the New England Ski Museum.*

The free museum, open noon–5 PM, tells the story of skiing in this area. On display are the amusement park ride–like Mount Cranmore Skimobile, which carried skiers from 1938 to 1987, and a single chairlift from Gunstock, which was used from 1938 to 1977. The entrance to the museum is through the original Cannon Mountain gondola, New England's first gondola, which was used from 1938 to 1980.

After exploring the museum, ride back to the bike path through the parking lot and turn right. At the stop sign, carefully cross US 3 and go left on the paved road.

1.32　*This portion of the bikeway is now shared by many walkers, so you must dismount and walk your bike. The trail goes left, crossing under busy I-93.*

On the right is an old log cabin, which is the Profile Lake Interpretive Center. It has exhibits on the birds of the Franconia Notch area, and on the glory days of the grand hotels.

1.65　*You reach the parking lot, where motorists stop to see the Old Man of the Mountain, a natural rock formation 1200 feet above you.*

In 1805, Francis Whitcomb and Luke Brooks, the first white men to see the structure, thought it resembled Thomas Jefferson. But in 1851, a Swedish writer, Fredericka Bremer, described the old man as not having "any nobility in its features, but resembles an old man in a bad humor."

Continuing on the trail, you cross a wooden bridge. Go under I-93 again, and encounter a marvelous downhill section with many picnic tables.

3.42 *You enter the parking lot for the Lafayette Place area and follow the bike-route signs to the right.*

In the middle is a cabin, which is the hiking center. In the meadow around the hiking center are signs that tell you of the geological history of Franconia Notch. This area offers views of 5248-foot Mount Lafayette and 5108-foot Mount Lincoln.

5.06 *At the Basin, you ride next to the Pemigewasset River.*

"Pemigewasset" is an Abenaki word that has been translated to mean either "swift" or "the crooked mountain pine place." Just below the path is a giant pothole called The Old Man's Foot. It's always been a popular spot; Thoreau visited here back in 1839. It's another section where your bike must be walked.

After a great downhill, you cross the Pemigewasset on a wooden bridge.

7.04 *After 40 minutes and a descent of 770 feet, you arrive at the parking lot for the Flume. Here the bike-route signs indicate a right turn, but you turn left for the Flume Visitor Center.*

7.14 *Reach the Flume Visitor Center.*

The Center is one of Franconia Notch's main attractions. It features a 2-mile walk through a spectacular 800-foot gorge with sheer 90-foot walls. You walk past waterfalls, pools, and glacial boulders. The center has a free 15-minute movie on the gorge's features. A $5.50 bus ride transports most visitors to the entrance of the gorge.

After the visitors center, go right through the parking lot.

7.30 Turn left onto unsigned US 3.

Although the recreational path ended at the Flume parking lot, US 3 has a wide, marked shoulder. This next highly commercialized section provides a good argument for creating public parks.

11.14 At the flashing light opposite Clark's Trading Post (the impossible-to-miss attraction opened in 1928), go left onto E-1.

12.12 At the T, go left onto NH 112.

14.37 Turn right into Loon Mountain Park.

14.54 You're back at the start.

11
Bretton Woods, New Hampshire

For over 175 years, outdoor enthusiasts have been attracted to the area around Mount Washington. Bretton Woods is a low-key resort that offers great mountain biking at all levels, including roads, singletracks, and terrain gardens. It has splendid views of Mount Washington and the beautiful Mount Washington Hotel. I never tire of watching the old steam trains laboring toward the highest point in New England. Bretton Woods features dining at the top of the lift and provides a gateway to the many attractions of the Crawford Notch/Mount Washington area.

In 1772, this area was granted to Sir Thomas Wentworth, the Rev. Samuel Langdon, and others as Britton Woods. But it was actually named after Bretton Hall, Sir Thomas's estate in Bretton, England. In 1832, it was incorporated as Carroll. But the name Bretton Woods was revived and is now applied to the region of the ski resort and the Mount Washington Hotel.

In 1819 Abel Crawford, the "patriarch of the White Mountains," and his son Ethan Allen Crawford constructed the first trail to the summit of 6288-foot Mount Washington. Together, in 1828, they erected the first Crawford House, which soon became a favorite with White Mountain visitors. While living there in 1846, Lucy Crawford published *The History of the White Mountains*, the area's first written record. The Crawford House was run by Ethan's brother, Thomas, until it was sold in 1852. Fires

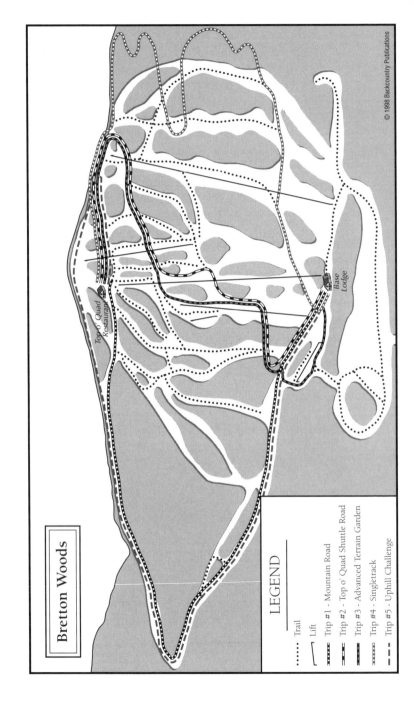

Bretton Woods

LEGEND

.... Trail
⌐   Lift
▨▨▨ Trip #1 - Mountain Road
▨▨▨ Trip #2 - Top o' Quad Shuttle Road
▨▨▨ Trip #3 - Advanced Terrain Garden
▨▨▨ Trip #4 - Singletrack
▬ ▬ ▬ Trip #5 - Uphill Challenge

Top o' Quad
Restaurant

Base
Lodge

© 1998 Backcountry Publications

in 1854 and 1859 destroyed the original inn and a replacement. Col. Cyrus Eastman erected the third Crawford House. It was prefabricated in neighboring towns and assembled over a period of nine months.

With its grand dining hall—having neither pillars nor posts—it opened in July 1859 to continue a tradition of hospitality to White Mountain visitors. Among them were Daniel Webster, Ralph Waldo Emerson, Washington Irving, Nathaniel Hawthorne, John Greenleaf Whittier, and Presidents Pierce, Grant, Hays, Garfield, and Harding.

The arrival of the railroad in 1875 made the journey even easier. You could have breakfast in Boston and dinner in the White Mountains. And New York was less than 12 hours away.

But an 1877 fire destroyed the Crawford House for the final time. Its carriage house was untouched by the flames and is today used by the Appalachian Mountain Club (AMC) as a storage facility. The AMC acquired the Shapleigh Studios and converted the building into the Crawford Notch Hostel. There hikers and cyclists can get a hot shower and a bed, just a few feet from the location of the original Crawford House.

The wonderfully maintained Mount Washington Hotel was the largest and most flamboyant of the resorts in the region. An early description shows it was definitely of a previous era: "There is a great ball room, a swimming pool . . . dining-rooms and tea-rooms for all the occasions the books of etiquette prescribe; the smartest New York shops [and] the leading brokerage houses."

At its 1902 dedication, the multimillionaire Joseph Stickney is supposed to have looked at his hotel, which some considered a folly, laughed, and said, "Look at me, gentlemen . . . for I am the poor fool who built all this!"

Before the Great Depression, the wealthy would spend their entire summers at the hotel, which rivaled resorts in Bar Harbor and Newport, bringing their servants with them. Fifty to sixty trains would arrive daily, and the sidings by the golf course would be filled with private railway cars.

In July 1944, the World Monetary Fund met at Bretton Woods and set the price of gold at $32 per ounce. This directly stabilized the post–World War II international economy and indirectly caused the dollar to be the currency standard for the world. The conference room used for this meeting is now a museum. Today, with over 300 rooms, dozens of outbuildings, and its own telephone exchange and post office, it is still the largest resort hotel in New England.

How to get there: Take I-93 to exit 35. Take US 3 north 11 miles to US 302, then take US 302 east 4 miles to Bretton Woods.

From I-95, take US 4 and NH 16 north 75 miles to US 302. Then take US 302 west 38 miles to Bretton Woods.

Total miles of biking available: 25 miles of trails plus 12 miles (20 km) cross-country.

The lift: The 15-minute ride to the top on a detachable quad takes you between groups of maple trees. Your bike rides up on the side of the chairlift on a bracket that holds the top tube. As you ride, a look to the left gives you a view of Mount Washington, on whose slopes you can see the smoke from the cog railroad engines as they take passengers from the 2569-foot base to the 6288-foot summit.

You can wash off your bike with a hose by the main lodge.

Season and hours: Weekends from Memorial Day to late June. Daily late June to mid-October, 10 AM–4:30 PM.

Prices: A single ride is $7; an all-day pass is $18.

Rental bikes: Front-suspension adult mountain bikes are $30 all day ($16 for 2 hours). Full-suspension mountain bikes are $39 all day, $24 for 2 hours. Front-suspension junior mountain bikes are $20 all day or $10 for 2 hours.

On the deck of the restaurant at Bretton Woods,
with Mount Washington in the background

Bike shop: Bretton Woods has a complete bike shop.

Trail identification: The trails are marked with orange circles.

Special features: Bretton Woods has two terrain gardens. These are the mountain bicycle equivalent of a snowboard park and feature challenging terrain, jumps, and balance beams.

There is a wonderful restaurant at the top of the lift, where you can eat lunch on the deck (11 AM–3 PM) while enjoying the views of Mount Washington.

Reservation number: 1-800-232-2972

Internet address: http://www.brettonwoods.com/summer.html #par2

E-mail address: skibw@brettonwoods.com

Hiking: Hikers can take the lift to the top and explore Bretton Woods by foot, including the Bretton Woods nature trail, or investigate the many trails in the Mount Washington region of the White Mountains.

Other activities: Mountain bike challenge, biathlon, and a dual slalom duel.

Festivals: Typical summer activities might include fireworks, a country music jamboree and craft fair, an ingenuity fair, and kids' alpine adventure.

Campgrounds: There are four campgrounds in Carroll, a few miles to the east: The Beach Hill Campground (603-846-5521) has 83 sites; the Ammonoosuc Campground (603-846-5527) has 75 sites; the Streams of Living Water Campground (603-846-5513) has 74 sites; and the Tarry-Ho Campground (603-846-5577) has 40 sites.

Hostel: The AMC operates several huts in the Mount Washington area. The Crawford Notch Hostel (603-466-2727), just off US 302 a few miles to the east, offers coed bunkhouses (heated in the winter months), showers, a self-service kitchen, educational displays, a library, and special programs.

Suggested itinerary

Warm up by descending on the easy trails and singletracks of:

Bretton Trip 1: Mountain Road

Distance: *1.75 miles*
Terrain: *Ski-area access roads and trails*
Difficulty: *Moderate*
Time: *15 minutes*
Elevation loss: *970 feet*

0.00   *From the top of the quad lift, go left (east) and ride underneath the restaurant, right across the lower porch, and enter the woods on a trail marked* MOUNTAIN ROAD *#19. You leave the woods and cross a ski run. At the junction with the Perimeter Trail, continue straight into the woods on Mountain Road, which passes the entrance to Bretton Woods' Nature Walk. Stay on Mountain Road, which varies between a singletrack and a trail. You then cross a wooden bridge and encounter a short muddy section.*

0.74   *After 7 minutes and 130 feet of descending, turn left to descend on the Two Miles Home ski run on a singletrack through the middle of a meadow.*

       (*Note:* Mountain Road continues straight ahead at this point, but is not part of the Bretton Woods area.)

       Now you cross a dirt road, which is the Top O' Quad run, and veer left onto a trail by the ROSEBROOK MEADOW *sign.*

1.75   *You're back at the lift.*

Now you're ready for a slightly harder ride, down dirt roads, that offers excellent views of Mount Washington:

Bretton Trip 2: Top O' Quad Shuttle Road

Distance: *1.62 miles*
Terrain: *Ski-area access roads and trails*
Difficulty: *Moderate*
Time: *13 minutes*
Elevation loss: *1060 feet*

0.00 *From the top of the quad lift, go right (west) onto the Top O' Quad road, signed EASY WAY DOWN, and almost immediately begin a slight ascent.*

As you ride by the top of the Mount Oscar double chairlift, the road curves to the right. At this point the trails to Coos Caper and Granny's Grit veer off to the left. This section of the road offers wonderful views of both Mount Washington and the beautiful Mount Washington Hotel.

0.85 *After 8 minutes and a descent of 430 feet, just underneath the quad, your road swings to the left by the entrance to the Upper Terrain Garden.*

This next section is quite steep and has a surface of loose, slippery gravel.

1.42 *Straight ahead the road is paved and leads into a parking lot for some condos. Here you veer left onto the Two Miles Home trail.*

1.62 *You're back at the bottom of the quad chairlift.*

Now you should be warmed up enough for the obstacle course of:

Bretton Trip 3: Advanced Terrain Garden

Distance: *1.75 miles*
Terrain: *Ski-area access roads and trails*
Difficulty: *Moderate*
Time: *15 minutes*
Elevation loss: *1080 feet*

0.00 *From the top of the quad lift, go right (west) onto the Top O'*
Quad road, signed EASY WAY DOWN, *and almost immediately*
begin a slight ascent.

As you ride by the top of the Mount Oscar double chairlift, the road curves to the right. At this point the trails to Coos Caper and Granny's Grit veer off to the left. This section of the road offers wonderful views of both Mount Washington and the beautiful Mount Washington Hotel.

0.85 *After 8 minutes and a descent of 430 feet, just underneath the*
quad, where the road swings to the left, go to the right by the
sign TO TERRAIN GARDEN. *Descend via a trail that runs through a*
meadow/ski run.

0.95 *After 8 minutes and a drop of 470 feet, enter the Advanced Ter-*
rain Garden.

This includes a balance beam, a slalom course, logs, and a rock garden. At the bottom of the ridge that serves as a half-pipe for snowboarders in winter, the trail turns to the right and snakes back and forth across the Bretton's Wood ski run.

Back underneath the quad, you turn right onto the Top O' Quad
work road.

1.47 *Straight ahead the road is paved; it leads into a parking lot for*
some condos. Here you veer left onto the Two Miles Home trail,
on which you immediately turn right at the ROSEBROOK MEADOW
and TO SLALOM COURSE *signs.*

1.75 *You're back at the lift, ready for another trip up.*

After lunch on the deck of the summit restaurant, you're probably ready for some singletrack activity on:

Bretton Trip 4: Singletrack
Distance: *1.84 miles*
Terrain: *Ski-area access roads and trails*
Difficulty: *Moderate*

Time: *22 minutes*
Elevation loss: *1070 feet*

*0.00   From the top of the quad lift, go right (west) onto the Top O'
Quad road, signed EASY WAY DOWN, and almost immediately
begin a slight ascent. Just past the top of the Mount Oscar
double chairlift, where the road begins to turn to the right, go
left into the trees onto the singletrack signed TRAIL and
SLOW/CAUTION.*

The singletrack is marked by orange trail signs on bamboo
poles, by pink tape, and by blue blazes on some trees.

*0.65   You leave the singletrack and veer to the left onto Glade West,
a narrow ski run, then veer right following the EASY WAY OUT
signs.*

*0.66   Still following the EASY WAY OUT sign, veer right and ride across a
ski run that offers a wonderful view of the beautifully restored
Mount Washington Hotel.*

*0.70   You enter another singletrack. When you exit from the trees, go
left onto a wide ski run. Keep descending the ski run with the
EASY WAY TO COOS CAPER sign.*

*0.78   Go left through a gap in the trees onto trail #1, Coos Caper.
After traversing a run, you enter another gap in the trees and
go to the right down a ski run.*

*1.19   You leave the narrow ski run, turn left, and descend a wide ski
run. Near the bottom of the ski run, with the highway visible, go
right through a gap in the trees. You traverse several ski runs;
then, with the quad lift right in front of you, go left and descend.
After crossing a little wooden bridge, go left directly under the
quad.*

1.84   You're back at the bottom of the quad.

The lift doesn't reach Bretton Woods' summit, but you can reach
it on:

Bretton Trip 5: Uphill Challenge

Distance: *2.58 miles*
Terrain: *Ski-area access roads and trails*
Difficulty: *Moderate*
Time: *25 minutes*
Elevation loss: *1290 feet*
Elevation gain: *300 feet*

0.00 *From the top of the quad lift, go right (west) onto the Top O'*
Quad road, signed EASY WAY DOWN, *and almost immediately*
begin a slight ascent.

0.20 *At the sign* UPHILL CHALLENGE #13, *go left and begin a steep*
climb, a walker for me in several places.

0.51 *After a gain of 300 feet, you reach a ridge just past the 2960-*
foot top of the Fabyan's Express double chairlift. From here you
have wonderful views of the entire Presidential Range. You leave
this area by taking the wider trail to the right of the PERIMETER
18 sign. Don't go down the very steep hill.

It's too bad that the lift doesn't go this high on the mountain, because this is perhaps the easiest way down, perfect for the novice mountain biker. This is a very slight descent, without enough speed to jump the frequent water bars.

Cross Mountain Road and keep descending straight on the Two
Miles Home trail. Then you cross the Top O' Quad dirt road and
continue straight down the trail, veering to the left by the ROSE-
BROOK MEADOW *sign.*

2.58 *You're at the base lodge once again.*

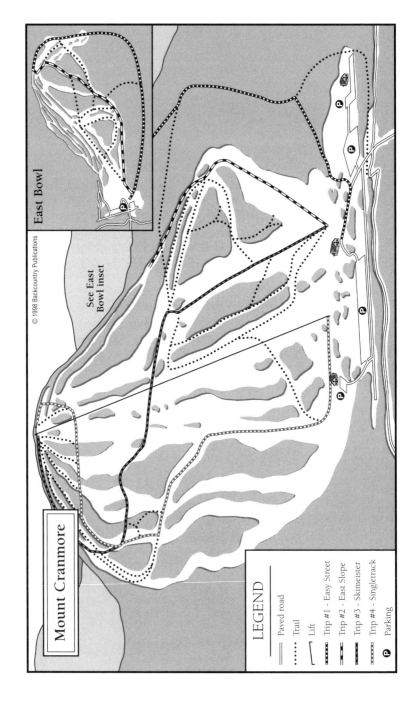

Mount Cranmore

East Bowl

See East
Bowl inset

© 1998 Backcountry Publications

LEGEND

Paved road
Trail
Lift
Trip #1 - Easy Street
Trip #2 - East Slope
Trip #3 - Skimeister
Trip #4 - Singletrack
Ⓟ Parking

12
Mount Cranmore, New Hampshire

The North Conway area features two resorts: Cranmore and Attitash Bear (see chapter 13). Both of these, along with Waterville Valley (chapter 14), used to be owned by the same outfit. When it expanded to become the American Skiing Company, though, it was required to sell Cranmore and Waterville.

For the serious mountain biker, Cranmore offers a true downhill experience. For the visitor who would like some easy cross-country mountain biking, with moderate downhills, Attitash Bear's truck shuttle to Bear Notch may be just the ticket. For the younger or noncycling members of the family, Cranmore's former sister resort, Attitash Bear, features an alpine slide, chairlift rides, a waterslide, a children's play pool, pony rides, a golf driving range, and horseback rides. For everyone, North Conway offers accommodations, dining, shopping, and access to the Mount Washington Valley.

Harvey Dow Gibson always thought that Lookout Mountain, near his hometown of North Conway, New Hampshire, could be developed into a ski resort that would not only allow visitors to realize the beauty of the area, but also provide employment in the Mount Washington Valley. In 1937, as the president of a major New York bank, he was able to make this dream happen, but he changed the name to Mount Cranmore.

One of the unique features of Cranmore was 1938's addition of the Skimobile (see Loon Trip 3, "Franconia Notch"). Skiers got to the top of the slope by riding one of the 180 cable-drawn cars, which had the look of a child's amusement park ride. But the Skimobile rocketed skiers to the top in a neck-snapping 20 minutes. Today's quad takes about half as much time to lift mountain bikers to the top, even at its reduced summer speed.

A year later, Gibson helped bring Hans Schneider, Austria's famed Skimeister, to Cranmore. Schneider is said to have skied before he walked and won his first race on a pair of barrel staves. Luckily, the prize was a pair of skis. He opened the world's first ski school in his homeland in 1907 and by the 1930s had become one of the most famous skiers in the world. He not only taught in the Alps, but ranged the world from Japan to New York City, spreading the word about skiing. His films, such as 1938's *Ski Chase*, helped to further popularize skiing in the United States.

But 1938 also brought the Anschluss: Hitler's annexation of Austria. Schneider refused to join the Nazis and was placed under house arrest. As a banker, Harvey Gibson realized that Germany owed the United States a sizable amount of money. He negotiated with the Nazis and was able to have Schneider released and sent to Mount Cranmore. On February 11, 1939, as Schneider and his family disembarked from the train in North Conway, about 150 local schoolchildren greeted them by forming an archway with their raised ski poles.

Schneider opened a ski school at Cranmore and may have done more to popularize skiing in the United States than anyone else. When he died, in 1955, so many accolades were sent to North Conway that extra personnel had to be hired by the tiny post office to handle the overload. He's buried in the small cemetery on Main Street, where his headstone says in German: "Rest in peace far from your homeland / Until we meet again." There is also a statue of the Skimeister in the parking lot at Cranmore, erected on its 50th anniversary.

How to get there: From I-95, take US 4 and NH 16 for 80 miles to North Conway. From I-93, take the Kancamagus Highway (NH 112) for 42 miles to North Conway, or US 302 for 54 miles to North Conway.

Total miles of biking available: 25+

The lift: You ride up on a four-person detachable quad chairlift. Your bike rides up on the side of the lift, on a hook that supports the frame. Your lift ticket is attached to your bike via an elastic cord, which seems too long. But it needs to be long, because you have to insert the lift ticket into a machine at a turnstile before each trip up the hill.

The trip to the top takes about 9^1/$_2$ minutes (in winter it takes about 5). As you pass through stands of maples, you can usually hear the whistle of the North Conway Scenic Railway. Below the lift, daisies and daylilies and a granite ledge compete for your attention.

On the way up you can see 3268-foot Kearsarge Mountain, the one on the left (north) with the fire lookout tower on its summit. The ledges behind you (west) are Whitehorse Ledge and Cathedral Ledge, popular with rock climbers. But it's 6288-foot Mount Washington, the highest peak in New Hampshire's Presidential Range, that dominates the view from both the lift and the valley below.

Season and hours: Weekends, Memorial Day through Columbus Day; daily, mid-June through Labor Day weekend, 10 AM–5 PM.

Prices: An all-day pass costs $18; two trips $12; a single trip $7.

Rental bikes: Adult: all-day $30 ($15 junior); half-day $20 ($15 junior); $7 per hour

Bike shop: Cranmore features a full-service bike shop.

Trail identification: Trails are marked with orange circles.

Special features: Cranmore also features the Descender, an adult scooter with suspension and disk brakes, which can

129

be rented for the day for $35 ($25 junior), or for a half-day for $20 ($12 junior). The Cranmore Sports Center (603-356-6301) features an indoor pool, sauna, Jacuzzi, tanning bed, aerobics, Nautilus, free weights, personal trainers, tennis, and a rock-climbing wall.

Reservation number: 1-800-223-SNOW (1-800-223-7669)

Internet address: http://www.cranmore.com/

Hiking: Hikers can take the chairlift to the top for $7 and then explore the Mount Cranmore area. The Mount Washington Valley's numerous peaks, including Mount Washington, attract hikers and climbers from around the world.

Other activities: When Cranmore opened in the late 1930s, the primary way to get there was via the railroad, with trains from Boston and New York arriving daily. That era is gone, but a reminder of those days is the Conway Scenic Railroad (603-356-5251 or 1-800-232-5251), whose whistles you can hear while on the mountain.

In the evening, Conway has theaters and restaurants. Nearby, in Bartlett, is Margaritaville, an excellent Mexican restaurant.

Festivals: Typical festivals might include a Blueberry Festival; an Equine Festival; a Rodeo and Powwow; the White Mountain Jazz & Blues Festival; and a Fall Festival.

Campgrounds: The Beach Camping Area (603-447-2723), Conway, has 120 sites; Eastern Slope Camping Area (603-447-5092), Conway, has 260 sites; Saco River Camping Area (603-356-3360), Conway, has 140 sites; Silver Springs (603-374-2221), Bartlett, has 52 sites; and the Glen-Ellis Family Campground (603-383-9320), Bartlett, has 128 sites.

Hostel: At the Albert B. Lester Memorial Hostel (36 Washington Street, Conway, 603-447-1011) you stay in an old farmhouse 6 miles to the south of Cranmore.

Suggested itinerary

Warm up by descending some uncomplicated roads and trails on the appropriately named:

Cranmore Trip 1: Easy Street

Distance: *2.91 miles*
Terrain: *Ski-area access roads and trails*
Difficulty: *Moderate*
Time: *30 minutes*
Elevation loss: *1130 feet*

0.00 From the top, you ride down the ramp and go left (north) on the trail marked SERVICE ROAD ACCESS TO OTHER TRAILS.

This is a dirt road that is sheltered by trees, so you don't get much of a view.

Bear right onto the road signed NOT A SKI TRAIL *and ride by the junction with the trails to Black Cap and Hurricane Mountain Road.*

Now you'll encounter a slight climb. You emerge from the trees in a meadow at bottom of the East Bowl Chairlift and then reenter the trees.

1.79 You've descended 720 feet in 15 minutes, and now the unmarked South Slope Connector trail merges from the right. You leave the road and veer right onto an unsigned trail, which leaves the shelter of the trees and passes just above the clay tennis courts of the Cranmore Sports Center. Go over a small wooden bridge, cross a stream, enter the main parking lot, and pass a bronze statue of Hans Schneider.

2.91 You're back at the lift.

Now you're ready to try something a little more challenging, a descent with views into the Mount Washington Valley:

Cranmore Trip 2: East Slope

Distance: 1.62 miles
Terrain: Ski-area access roads and trails
Difficulty: Moderate
Time: 20 minutes
Elevation loss: 1090 feet

0.00 *From the top, you ride down the ramp and go right (south) on the trail marked* EAST SLOPE TO SCHNEIDER AND GIBSON. *At the T, turn left onto the signed* BIKE TRAIL.

You pass under a ski lift line, where the trail narrows to a singletrack through a meadow. From a clearing in the trees you can see into the Mount Washington Valley.

At the TO SCHNEIDER AND ARTIST FALLS TRAILS *sign, you enter a woods of maple and birch.*

0.87 *Having descended 640 feet in 10 minutes, you veer left at a junction in a meadow by the* BEGINNER'S LUCK *sign. Then at the bottom of a ski run, traverse the slope to the right.*

1.62 *You reach the bottom of the lift.*

You may want to try some of the trails on the northern side of the resort, such as:

Cranmore Trip 3: Skimeister

Distance: 1.58 miles
Terrain: Ski-area access roads and trails
Difficulty: Moderate
Time: 30 minutes
Elevation loss: 1100 feet

0.00 *From the top, ride down the ramp and go left (north) toward the ski patrol hut. Turn left onto the trail signed* RATTLESNAKE TRAIL, SKIMEISTER TRAIL, KANDAHAR TRAIL *and immediately veer right onto the unsigned Kandahar Trail. Then immediately bear left; at*

Mount Cranmore, New Hampshire

   the junction with an unmarked trail, veer left again.

0.42 You encounter a clearing through the trees that offers a wonderful view into the Mount Washington Valley, and then merge with a trail from the left and begin to traverse a ski slope.

0.74 After dropping 490 feet in 15 minutes, you traverse the main runs under the quad and then climb slightly. You'll encounter a very sandy turn to the right and then ride to the right of the upper lift tower. Beyond the tower, go left and descend on a singletrack through a meadow.

1.58 You're back at the start.

Now it's time for lunch, perhaps at the Meister Hut, Cranmore's summit restaurant. After lunch you're ready to tackle Cranmore's most difficult trail, a singletrack with technical sections through mud and over slippery rock outcroppings:

Cranmore Trip 4: Singletrack

Distance: 1.57 miles
Terrain: Ski-area access roads and trails
Difficulty: Moderate
Time: 25 minutes
Elevation loss: 1090 feet

0.00 From the top, ride down the ramp and go to the far right (south) onto the trail marked TO LEDGES AND KOESSLER TRAILS. EXPERT ONLY.

Note: The same trail has a bike sign marked PREMIER (SINGLE-TRACK) AROUND MEISTER HUT.

Veer to the left of the Meister Hut, Cranmore's summit restaurant, then go right on the trail signed EXPERT TRAIL. NO BEGINNERS. You go left and descend steeply (a walker for me) past some pine trees. Go right and over the granite ledges and under the quad, then you'll encounter a technical uphill section. At the T with the SKIMEISTER/SINGLETRACK sign, you go left on a singletrack.

0.56 Go left on the Skimeister ski run, then immediately turn right onto another singletrack.

0.69 At the T, after descending 380 feet in 17 minutes, you go left, emerge from the cover of the trees, and go straight down a ski run, now a meadow.

1.57 After riding by a pond that attracts ducks and other wildlife, a source of water for the snowmaking machines in winter, you arrive at the lift.

13
Attitash Bear, New Hampshire

Although Attitash Bear doesn't offer lift-accessed mountain biking, there are several ways to benefit from its attractions: For many vacationers, taking the shuttle and riding a bike from Bear Notch Pass would satisfy any mountain biking desires. For families, Attitash Bear's golf driving range, alpine slide, chairlift rides, waterslide, children's play pool, pony rides, and horseback rides may serve as an all-day attraction for the non–mountain biking members of a family, while the cyclists drive or ride to its former sister resort, Cranmore, and enjoy its lift-accessed cycling. In the evening, everybody can enjoy the restaurants and shopping in North Conway.

How to get there: Attitash Bear is 10 miles from Cranmore (see chapter 12) on NH 16 and US 302.
Total miles of biking available: 7.75
Season and hours: Memorial Day to early June and Labor Day through Columbus Day: weekends 10 AM–5 PM. Mid-June through Labor Day: daily 10 AM–6 PM.
Prices: One ride on the shuttle is $5 per person.
Rental bikes: Mountain bikes can be rented for $30 per day ($15 juniors), $20 for a half-day ($7 junior), or $7 per hour.
Bike shop: There is a full-service pro shop at Attitash Bear.
Trail identification: Trails on the Bear Notch area are signed by red arrows.

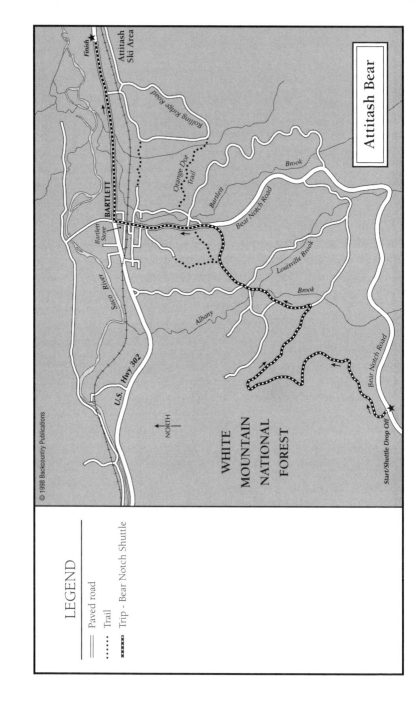

LEGEND

Paved road
Trail
Trip - Bear Notch Shuttle

Attitash Bear

Finish
Attitash Ski Area

Rolling Ridge Road

Orange Dot Trail

Brook

Bartlett

BARTLETT

Bartlett Store

Bear Notch Road

Louisville Brook

Brook

Saco River

Albany

Bear Notch Road

U.S. Hwy 302

NORTH

WHITE MOUNTAIN NATIONAL FOREST

Start/Shuttle Drop Off

© 1998 Backcountry Publications

Reservation number: 1-800-223-SNOW (1-800-223-7669)

Internet address: http://www2.attitash.com/attitash/summer/indexs.html

E-mail address: info@attitash.com

Hiking: A single ride to the summit on the chairlift is $7 ($5.50 junior).

Other activities: Golf driving range, alpine slide, scenic chair rides, water slides, Buddy Bear playpool, pony rides, and horseback riding.

Festivals: Typical festivals include the Mount Washington Valley Cup Soccer Tournament, the Blueberry Festival, the Attitash Bear Peak Equine Festival, Rodeo and Intertribal Pow Wow, Jazz and Blues Festival, and a Fall Festival.

Campgrounds: The Beach Camping Area (603-447-2723), Conway, has 120 sites; Eastern Slope Camping Area (603-447-5092), Conway, has 260 sites; Saco River Camping Area (603-356-3360), Conway, has 140 sites; Silver Springs (603-374-2221), Bartlett, has 52 sites; and the Glen-Ellis Family Campground (603-383-9320), Bartlett, has 128 sites.

Suggested itinerary

You and your bike take a shuttle (or you can ride your bike) to the top of paved Bear Notch Pass, then make the easy descent back to Attitash Bear on dirt and paved roads:

Attitash Trip 1: Bear Notch Shuttle

Distance: *7.75 miles*
Terrain: *Dirt road and paved highway*
Difficulty: *Moderate*
Time: *40 minutes*
Elevation loss: *1180 feet*

Attitash Bear, New Hampshire

0.00   *Begin descending the dirt road. Soon you encounter a slight climb and cross a brook.*

2.80   *At the Y, after descending 720 feet in 14 minutes, go left following the red arrows. Then, at a T, you'll go right, following the red arrows.*

3.44   *At a junction, go straight, cross a brook, and pass a blue water tank on your right. Keep going straight at the next two junctions.*

4.31   *Turn left onto Bear Notch Road, a paved highway.*

5.16   *After dropping 1080 feet in 30 minutes, you arrive at the community of Bartlett.*

The store on the left has an ice cream stand.

Make a right turn onto US 302.

7.75   *You're back at Attitash Bear.*

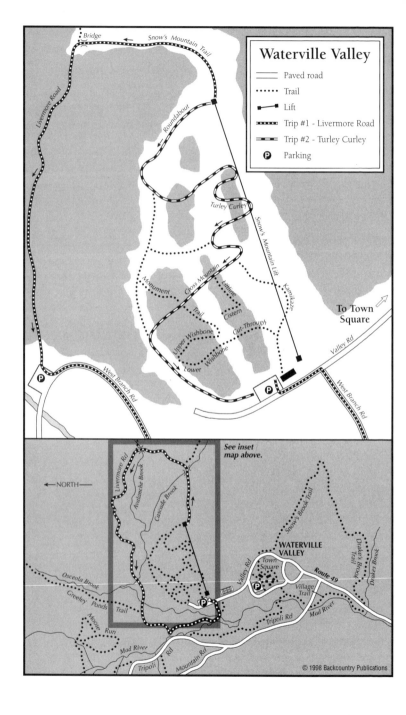

Waterville Valley

- Paved road
- .... Trail
- ■—•—■ Lift
- ••••• Trip #1 - Livermore Road
- ■—■—■ Trip #2 - Turley Curley
- Ⓟ Parking

Bridge
Snow's Mountain Trail
Livermore Road
Roundabout
Turley Curley
Monument
Cross Mountain Trail
Cistern
Cut-Through
Upper Wishbone
Lower Wishbone
Snow's Mountain Lift
Kamikaze
To Town Square
Valley Rd
West Branch Rd
West Branch Rd
Ⓟ
Ⓟ

See inset map above.

←NORTH

Livermore Rd
Avalanche Brook
Cascade Brook
Snow's Brook Trail
WATERVILLE VALLEY
Town Square
Drake's Brook Trail
Drakes Brook
Valley Rd
Route 49
Village Trail
Osceola Brook
Greeley Ponds Trail
Moose Run
Mad River
Tripoli Rd
Mountain Rd
Tripoli Rd
Mad River

© 1998 Backcountry Publications

14

Waterville Valley, New Hampshire

Waterville Valley is a hidden treasure. Tucked away in a valley that shields it from the same interstate that provides easy access, it offers all the amenities of a vacation destination: condos, restaurants, and shopping in a picturesque village—all a few minutes from the lift via a bike path. If it's too low key for you, the many commercial attractions of Lincoln are only a few minutes away.

If you reach Waterville Valley via paved NH 49, the approach is like that to many other resorts. But if you take unpaved Tripoli Road, you may think you've made a wrong turn. I couldn't believe that a resort would be located at the end of the dirt road, but soon realized that Waterville Valley is a world all its own.

Cut by New Hampshire's Mad River, Waterville Valley has attracted vacationers since the 1830s. A Christian hotel, built in 1868, drew ministers and teachers. In the 1910s their descendants bought the hotel and its surrounding 26,000 acres. They donated all the land but a few hundred acres to the Forest Service. The major trails were cut by Civilian Conservation Corps workers in the 1930s.

In 1965 Tom Corcoran, a former member of the Dartmouth ski team, purchased the hotel and 425 acres and began turning it into today's four-season resort. It is now operated by the owners of Vail, in Colorado.

Waterville Valley, with all its amenities, might be too civilized for some, but for many mountain bikers it's the definition of the sport. They rent bikes at the Village Square, ride the paved bike path ½ mile to the lift, experience off-road cycling on Livermore Road, and ride back to Village Square.

And yet Waterville Valley is challenging enough that at least one pro downhill rider calls it home.

How to get there: From I-93 north, take exit 28 to paved NH 49 and drive 11 miles to Waterville Valley. Don't turn left at the TO SKI AREA sign, but turn right on Valley Road, at the TO MOUNTAIN BIKE PARK sign. The Mountain Bike Park is 0.4 mile on the right. From I-93 south, take exit 31 and go 10 miles east on mostly unpaved Tripoli Road to Waterville Valley.

Total miles of biking available: 20+

The lift: The 12-minute ride to the top is on a double chairlift. Your bike hangs from the rear wheel on a separate chair.

From the lift you can see the clay courts of the tennis club to the right. You'll ride past stands of birch, ash, pine, and maple trees. Behind you is 4004-foot Mount Tecumseh, the summit of Waterville Valley's other ski area.

Season and hours: The lift is open weekends and holidays Memorial Day through Columbus Day, 9 AM–4 PM.

Prices: A full-day pass on the chairlift is $20 ($16 for juniors). A trail pass is $6.

Rental bikes: Rental bikes are available at Mountain Valley Bikes (603-236-4666) in the Waterville Valley town square for $40 per day, including an all-day lift pass.

Bike shop: Mountain Valley Bikes is in the town square.

Special features: One mile southwest of the Waterville Valley ski area, via a paved bikeway or road, is the Waterville Valley Village Square. Shops, restaurants, and a general store all overlook a small lake, where canoes, Sunfish sailboats, and paddleboats can be rented.

Trail identification: Trails are marked by a combination of permanent wooden signs and laminated plastic signs.

Reservation number: 603-236-4666

Internet address: http://www.waterville.com/biking.html

E-mail address: info@waterville.com

Hiking: There are many hiking trails in the area signed WVAIA. This means they are maintained by the Waterville Valley Athletic Improvement Association. One trip up the chairlift for hikers is $5 for adults; $4 for children. Guided hikes are offered daily at 9 AM for $9 per person. You can also hike to the summit of Mount Tecumseh, whose lifts are closed in summer.

Rider's comment: "Great riding and hiking for all levels, from kids to crazies."

Other activities: The Waterville Valley Base Camp is the center for all outdoor activities (except golf and tennis) and describes itself as "nature's own theme park." Besides mountain biking and hiking, it offers an introduction to orienteering for $19 per group. The Waterville Valley Sports Dome is an indoor facility offering in-line skating, skateboarding, and a climbing wall. It's open daily from late June to early September and weekends from early September through Columbus Day.

In the evening you can have dinner at the Village Square, or take the 30-minute drive to Lincoln for a wide variety of entertainment.

Campgrounds: The National Forest Service (603-536-1310) maintains Waterville, a primitive campground with 27 sites, at Waterville Valley; and Compton Campground, with 58 sites, located 2 miles east of I-93 on NH 49. The Forest Service also permits off-road camping at many spots along Tripoli Road. The Branch Brook campground (603-726-7001), located 1 mile west of I-93 on NH 49, has 150 sites.

The view of Mount Tecumseh from the bike trails at Waterville Valley

Suggested itinerary

Many resorts label runs as "easy way down" that are in reality "white knucklers" for the novice mountain biker. At Waterville Valley, you start out on a run that has stream crossings, waterfalls, and lots of side trips on WVAIA trails, but it's so easy that you'll see lots of people actually *riding* up:

Waterville Trip 1: Livermore Road

Distance: *4.46 miles*
Terrain: *Ski-area access roads and trails*
Difficulty: *Moderate*
Time: *30 minutes*
Elevation loss: *640 feet*

0.00 *You leave the lift and immediately veer right into the woods on a trail, shared with hikers, signed* EASIEST.

0.78 *Ride over the Cascade Brook on a wooden bridge from which you can see falls and swimming holes to your right.*

1.34 *Having gradually descended 290 feet in 10 minutes, you cross Avalanche Brook on another wooden bridge and turn left onto Livermore Road.*

2.68 *Ride by the Keetles Trail, then the Big Pines Path and the Boulder Path, all hiking trails that can be explored on a bicycle.*

Another wooden bridge takes you across Osceola Brook; on the right is the trail to Greeley Ponds.

3.64 *You ride around a locked gate, blocking motorized access to Livermore Road, and ride past a parking area. Don't ride across the wooden bridge, but go left onto paved, unsigned West Branch Road, an easy downhill section that crosses a wooden bridge spanning the west branch of the Mad River. After a short, steep climb, turn left on Boulder Way.*

4.46 *After a gradual descent, you're back at the start.*

At this point, perhaps you're ready for a singletrack with some mud and slippery rocks:

Waterville Trip 2: Turley Curley

Distance: *0.65 mile*
Terrain: *Ski-area access roads and trails*
Difficulty: *Moderate*
Time: *7 minutes*
Elevation loss: *620 feet*

0.00 *You leave the lift and immediately go left onto the Roundabout trail through a meadow. Turn left into the woods on unsigned Turley Curley, which exits the woods, traverses a ski run, reenters the trees, and goes right underneath the chairlift.*

0.36 *Where the Kamikaze trail continues under the lift, go right onto Turley Curley, then you veer right into the woods on the Cross Mountain trail, a narrow trail, almost singletrack in width, which is muddy and goes over slippery rocks.*

0.65 *You're back at the start.*

15
Mount Sunapee, New Hampshire

In the summers before air conditioning, the wealthy would flee the sweltering Eastern cities to cooler mountain areas, such as Lake Sunapee. The arrival of the railroads allowed more people to visit and large hotels were built to accommodate them. Steam-powered boats transported vacationers to various lakeside attractions during what became known as the era of the grand hotels.

Times changed and automobiles allowed the middle classes to enjoy the region. But the convenience of the automobile caused the railroads, the steam boats, and the grand hotels to disappear. The new visitors preferred to stay in smaller cottages or farmhouses and began to buy their own homes as summer residences. As skiing became popular, people heated their summer homes, and today's four-season resort area was born.

The lodge at Sunapee's 2743-foot summit is surrounded by decks that offer views to the east, west, and south. On the western deck is a pair of coin-operated binoculars. The peak 35 miles south of Sunapee is 3165-foot Mount Monadnock.

Sunapee has cut no singletracks through the woods, and its three trails down the mountain are some of the easiest descents in this book. But it also offers some of the most amazing views in the northeast. Therefore, it makes a great introduction to downhill mountain biking for the entire family.

During its very popular foliage weekends, the reaction of hikers coming down on the lift to mountain cyclists being given a ride up the mountain makes you feel like a hero.

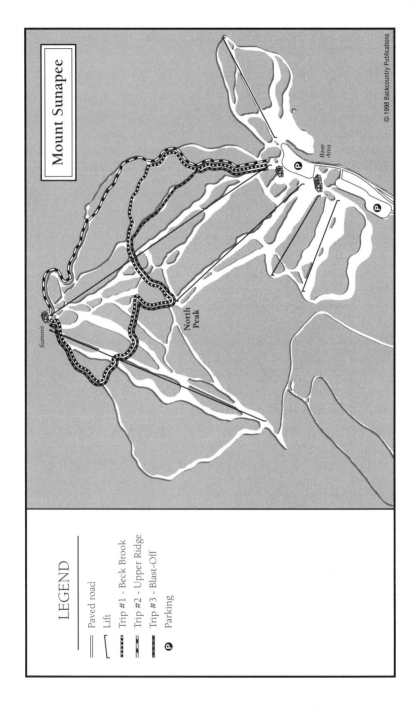

Mount Sunapee

LEGEND

- ═ Paved road
- [Lift
- Trip #1 - Beck Brook
- Trip #2 - Upper Ridge
- Trip #3 - Blast-Off
- **P** Parking

Summit

North Peak

Base Area

© 1998 Backcountry Publications

Mount Sunapee is operated by the New Hampshire Department of Resources and Economic Development.

How to get there: From I-89 north, take Exit 9 and follow NH 103 west for 16 miles. Mount Sunapee is on the left just after the town of Newbury. From I-91 take Exit 8 to NH 103 east through Claremont and Newport to Mount Sunapee State Park.

The lift: Mount Sunapee uses a triple chairlift to get you to the summit. On my first trip up, the lift operator let several cyclists ahead of the hikers who were in line at the chairlift. I thought, "Wow, this place really caters to the cyclist!" But in reality only 20 of the 222 chairs have bike racks, so if you're there when a chair with a bike rack is available you go to the front of the line. Otherwise, you wait until a chair with a rack arrives.

Mount Sunapee's lift operates at two speeds: very fast and very slow. About 55 or 60 chairs are loaded at the slow speed, then the lift is switched to the high speed. As these chairs near the top, the lift is again slowed down to let people off. The result is a 20- to 25-minute ascent. The lift operators say that without this two-speed technique, the trip would take about 45 minutes.

As you ascend on a clear day, you can see 6228-foot Mount Washington in the distance to the northeast. To the west, 3150-foot Mount Ascutney rises by itself from the floor of the Connecticut River Valley.

Season and hours: Daily, 9 AM–4 PM, July 1 to September 1. Call first for weekend hours in September and October.

Prices: An all-day lift ticket is $15; one trip up is $8.

Rental bikes: Bikes can be rented from Bob Skinner's Ski and Sport Shop at the traffic circle where the Mount Sunapee access road meets NH 103 (603-763-2303).

Bike shop: Bob Skinner's Ski and Sport

Trail identification: Trails open to mountain bikes are identified by a white sign featuring the picture of an old high-wheeled bicycle.

Special features: Mount Sunapee has a cafeteria in both the lower lodge and at the summit. On most summer weekends a barbecue is also available at the summit.

Reservation number: 1-800-258-3530 or 603-763-2356

Internet address: http://www.mtsunapee.com

E-mail address: info@mtsunapee.com

Hiking: A round-trip lift ticket is $5 for adults; $2.50 for children 6–12; free for children 5 and under. A one-way ticket is $4.50. Mount Sunapee has numerous trails and is the northern terminus for the 50-mile Monadnock-Sunapee Greenway Trail.

Other activities: You can swim at the beach at Lake Sunapee or rent a canoe or paddleboat. You can visit some of the 16 covered bridges in the greater Sunapee area. You can travel back into the era of the steamboat by taking a trip on the MV *Mount Sunapee II* (603-763-4030). Try kayaking at Shoreline Kayaking in Goshen (603-863-4017). Learn to scuba dive at Lake Sunapee with La Porte's Skindiving (603-763-5353). Or take in a play at the New London Playhouse (603-526-4631).

Festivals and attractions: These include the Lake Sunapee Business Association Flea Market and the Mount Sunapee 5K hill climb in July; the Gem & Mineral Show and the League of New Hampshire Craftsmen Craft Fair in August; the Audubon Society of New Hampshire Naturefest in September; and the Taste of New Hampshire Food Products Fair and the Mount Sunapee Cross-Country Foot Race in October.

Campground: The Rand Pond Campground in Goshen (603-863-3350) has 65 sites. The Otter Pond Campground in New

Mount Sunapee, New Hampshire

London (603-763-5600) has 28 sites. The Wildwood Forest Campground in Springfield (603-763-2057) has 26 sites. The Loon Lake Campground in Newport (603-863-8176) has 118 sites.

Suggested Itinerary

Before you take the easiest trail at Sunapee you are warned that it involves some climbing. But it's a climb that's almost over before you've had a chance to engage your low gears. Nevertheless you'll enjoy the views on:

Sunapee Trip 1: Beck Brook

Distance: *2.35 Miles*
Terrain: *Ski-area access roads and trails*
Difficulty: *Easy to moderate*
Time: *30 Minutes*

Elevation loss: *1420 Feet*
Elevation gain: *60 Feet*

0.00   Leaving the lift, you go left following the ALL TRAILS *sign.*

0.06   At the EASIER ROUTE *sign, go right following the* BIKE TRAIL *sign.*

0.27   Where the narrow Solitude Trail is straight ahead, cyclists must go left onto a wider ski run.

0.37   You go left where the PORKY *sign points to the right.*

0.65   You begin a moderate climb, which Sunapee describes as a singletrack.

Although it's not a true singletrack, it's just slightly narrower than their other trails.

1.07   After descending 510 feet in 20 minutes, the trail continues to the left.

1.33   You ride under the main lift.

1.42   At the BLAST-OFF *sign, veer left.*

1.80   You merge with the Upper Ridge trail.

2.35   After descending 1420 feet in 30 minutes, you're back at the lodge.

Now you may be ready for Sunapee's most difficult trail, although almost anywhere else it would be classified as the easiest way down. Regardless, enjoy yourself on:

Sunapee Trip 2: Upper Ridge

Distance: *1.73 Miles*
Terrain: *Ski-area access roads and trails*
Difficulty: *Easy to moderate*
Time: *17 Minutes*
Elevation loss: *1360 Feet*

0.00   Leaving the lift, you go left following the ALL TRAILS *sign.*

0.07   Go left at the EASIER TRAILS *sign.*

As you pass under the chairlift, Rand Pond is the body of water that is directly ahead of you. The peak to the right is Mount Ascutney. The trail makes a wide, sweeping turn to the right. Now you've entered an area where you must slow down to negotiate a series of rocky bumps; this is the closest thing to a technical section at Mount Sunapee.

1.34 *Veer right onto a ski run, which is a connector to Lower Blast-off.*

1.45 *You merge with the Beck Brook trail.*

1.73 *After descending 1360 feet in 16 minutes, you're back at the bottom.*

Now if you're ready for a break, ride the lift back to the summit and savor a meal on the deck of the lodge as you take in Sunapee's spectacular views. Then enjoy a third route down on:

Sunapee Trail 3: Lower Blast-Off

Distance: *2.30 Miles*
Terrain: *Ski-area access roads and trails*
Difficulty: *Easy to moderate*
Time: *35 Minutes*
Elevation loss: *1410 feet*
Elevation gain: *60 feet*

0.00 *Leaving the lift, you go left following the ALL TRAILS sign.*

0.06 *At the EASIER ROUTE sign, go right following the BIKE TRAIL sign.*

0.21 *You traverse a ski run which offers a marvelous view of Lake Sunapee.*

0.27 *Where the narrow Solitude Trail is straight ahead, cyclists must go left onto a wider ski run.*

0.37 *You go left where the PORKY sign points to the right.*

0.65 *You begin a moderate climb.*

153

1.07 After descending 510 feet in 20 minutes, the trail continues to the left.

But you may want to ride out to the top of the ski lift for a view of Lake Sunapee. It's a great place to sit and watch the sailboats.

1.17 You're back on the main trail again.

1.43 You ride under the main lift.

1.52 At the BLAST-OFF sign, go right onto a run.

A grassy meadow in summer, this run offers great views of Lake Sunapee and the surrounding hillsides.

2.01 You merge with the Upper Ridge and Beck Brook trails.

2.30 Having descended 1410 feet in 35 minutes, you're back at the bottom.

16
Sunday River, Maine

Sunday River lives up to its fine reputation. It's a long drive from the interstate, but well worth it. It has golf, tennis, and other attractions, but when you're there, you feel that mountain biking is king. Two lifts and an extensive network of downhill trails, singletracks, and cross-country trails offer a wide variety of riding. There are accommodations and restaurants, but if you're looking to shop when the trails close, you will be disappointed. Bethel (the closest town to Sunday River) is a typical New England village, not an artificial one created for the visitor, and wants to stay that way.

Sunday River opened in 1959, but it became a major resort with snowmaking and condominiums when it was acquired by The American Skiing Company, which also owns Killington.

Bethel is 6 miles to the south. It was settled in 1768 as Sudbury-Canada, but was renamed Bethel (meaning "house of God") in 1796. Up until 1851, Bethel was a sleepy farming town. In that year, however, the Atlantic and Saint Lawrence Railroad's route between Portland and Montréal enabled residents to transport lumber economically to distant markets. But the railroad also brought summer tourists, who came from cities to explore the White Mountains.

A reminder of this earlier era is the Bethel Inn, which opened in 1913 as a health spa. Part of the original regimen was strenuous exercise. The visitors actually paid the Bethel Inn for the privilege of splitting its firewood. You're no longer required to

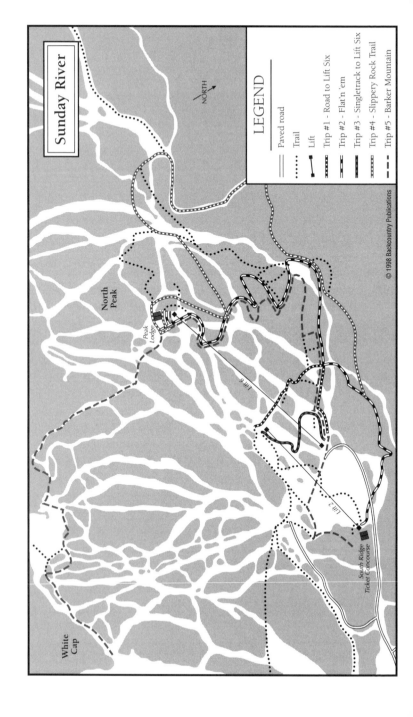

Sunday River

North
Peak

Peak
Lodge

Lift 6

Lift 2

South Ridge
Ticket Concourse

White
Cap

NORTH

LEGEND

Paved road

Trail

Lift

Trip #1 - Road to Lift Six

Trip #2 - Flat'n 'em

Trip #3 - Singletrack to Lift Six

Trip #4 - Slippery Rock Trail

Trip #5 - Barker Mountain

© 1998 Backcountry Publications

cut wood, but the Bethel Inn today is still a great place to eat breakfast in an elegant atmosphere before heading out onto Sunday River's trails.

Sunday River was the first resort in the East to offer lift-accessed mountain biking and four years ago became the first resort to provide two chairlifts.

How to get there: Take I-91 to Saint Johnsbury, Vermont. Follow US 2 east 67 miles to Bethel, Maine. From Bethel, follow the signs 6 miles north to Sunday River.

Or take I-95 to exit 11 (Gray, Maine). Pick up ME 26 to Norway/South Paris and continue to Bethel. Follow signs to US 2 east and Sunday River.

Total miles of biking available: 40+

The lift: Sunday River is the only resort in this book that features two chairlifts for mountain bikers. Lift #2 is a detachable quad, while Lift #6 is a triple chairlift. On both you ride up on a different chair than your bike does. Your bike rides up on the back of the chair on a rack made from rebar. Sunday River is the only resort with warning signs on the lift poles aimed at mountain bike riders.

Season and hours: The Sunday River Mountain Bike Park is open weekends beginning Memorial Day weekend, and daily from July 4th through Labor Day. From Labor Day through Columbus Day, Sunday River is open daily, but the lifts operate only on weekends. Sunday River is open 9 AM–4 PM, with the lift running until 3 PM.

Prices: An all-day pass is $22; a season pass is $150. A single lift ride for hikers is $8. An all-day trail pass and one lift ride costs $17. Helmet rentals are $5.

Rental bikes: Full-suspension mountain bikes, including lift ticket and helmet, are $45 per day. Lighter, professional-level, full-suspension mountain bikes, including lift ticket and helmet, are $50 per day.

Bike shop: There is a full-service bike shop in the base lodge. Spare tubes and a foot pump are available at the top of Lift #6.

Trail identification: Trails at Sunday River are marked by wooden mountain bike trail signs.

Special features: Sunday River is one of two resorts in this book that have two lifts open in the summer and that rents the Descender CX-10, a sort of big-wheeled scooter.

Or you can try the Terrain Garden in front of the South Ridge Lodge. It has all the turns, jumps, and obstacles of the mountain in one area. Two-hour Learn to Mountain Bike clinics are $30, and 3-hour guided tours are offered each afternoon for $20 per person.

Reservation number: 1-800-543-2SKI

Internet address: http://sundayriver.com/bike (*Note:* Bethel has its own home page at: http://www.nxi.com/WWW/bethel/homepage.html)

E-mail address: snowtalk@sundayriver.com

Hiking: Hikers can take the lift to the top and hike down or enjoy any of the many other trails in the region.

Rider's comment: "Sunday River is way more organized than Sugarloaf, with better restaurants and food, better lodging, and a location closer to the interstate."

Other activities: The Sunday River area also offers guided canoe trips, fishing, Camp Sunday River for children, golf, shopping in Bethel, a four-screen cinema in Bethel, and the Sunday River Brewing Company.

Campground: The Stony Brook Recreation area in Newry (207-824-2836) has 25 sites.

Suggested itinerary

After breakfast at the nearby Bethel Inn, how about an easy route from Lift #2 to Lift #6:

Sunday Trip 1: Road to Lift Six

Distance: *0.72 mile*
Terrain: *Ski-area access roads and trails*
Difficulty: *Moderate*
Time: *3 minutes*
Elevation loss: *320 feet*

0.00 From the top of Lift #2, go right on the dirt road.

0.37 Turn right at the junction signed TO LIFT #6.

0.72 You're at the bottom of Lift #6.

Here's a trail that combines dirt roads and moderate singletracks:

Sunday Trip 2: Flat'n 'em

Distance: *3.10 miles*
Terrain: *Ski-area access roads and trails*
Difficulty: *Moderate*
Time: *20 minutes*
Elevation loss: *1190 feet*

0.00 From the top of Lift #6, go left and ride by the Peak Lodge, which is usually closed in summer. At the next clearing, go left following the TO FLAT'N 'EM 20 sign.

0.11 At the T, turn left onto Flat'n 'em.

0.85 At the junction where #12 Moose Tack goes to the right, go left on Flat'n 'em and cross two bridges.

The first is short; the second requires you to maintain your balance, as the bridge actually twists.

1.02 After descending 580 feet in 10 minutes, you go right onto #21 Aurora Peak Road, which is rough in places.

1.61 At the stop sign, turn left onto #7 Ridge Run, which goes left, and climb into the woods. Just before some condos, go left into the woods for a surprisingly nice section of singletrack with both

> *bumps and bridges. Then leave the singletrack and turn right onto a trail.*

2.48 You veer right across a bridge that crosses a paved road.

3.10 You're back at the main area.

You've tried the most direct route from Lift #2 to Lift #6—here's one that's more fun:

Sunday Trip 3: Singletrack to Lift #6

Distance: *0.61 mile*
Terrain: *Ski-area access roads and trails*
Difficulty: *Moderate*
Time: *5 minutes*
Elevation loss: *350 feet*

0.00 After getting off Lift #2, walk your bike down the ramp and go to the right on the wide road. Almost immediately, go right onto the singletrack signed SR2.

SR2 enters the trees, veers left through the trees to go under Lift #2, climbs to the left through the trees, traverses a ski run into some more woods, crosses a little bridge, traverses another ski run, and crosses another little bridge.

0.38 The trail becomes SR6.

SR6 passes through a fairly technical section, emerges from the woods, and becomes the dirt road to the right.

0.61 You're at Lift #6, ready to ride to the summit of the upper mountain.

You'll think you've been transported to Utah on:

Sunday Trip 4: Slippery Rock Trail

Distance: *4.39 miles*
Terrain: *Ski-area access roads and trails*

Difficulty: *Moderate*
Time: *40 minutes*
Elevation loss: *1390 feet*

0.00   *From the top of Lift #6, go left and ride by the Peak Lodge, which is usually closed in summer. At the clearing next to the restaurant, go right following #14 Upper Catch 'em.*

0.41   *You ride over the exposed granite of the "slippery rock"–type section.*

Wear a pair of orange sunglasses and you can imagine you're in Utah.

0.52   *Go left onto Flat'n 'em, a wide road.*

0.54   *At the junction, veer left onto Sensation.*

1.02   *Here you go left onto Catch 'em and begin a slight climb.*

1.56   *After a 120-foot climb, you reach the bottom of a lift, which is the Jordan Bowl ski area. Here you take the road that veers to the right through the trees.*

1.91   *At this junction, you follow the signed CATCH 'EM trail to the right, which makes a sharp turn to the left, takes you through a muddy spot, and narrows into a singletrack.*

2.59   *After a descent of 810 feet in 20 minutes, turn right onto unsigned #15 Cut 'em Off, which crosses a brook on a small bridge. After a tough climb up a rocky slope, go left at a junction of two unsigned trails.*

3.08   *After encountering a very steep climb of 120 feet, you go left on the road, which is Aurora Peak Road.*

3.37   *To make the descent a little more interesting, leave the road and go left onto the Keep It Going singletrack.*

3.66   *Go left onto the unsigned Ridge Road.*

3.78   *You climb up the trail, which goes to the right.*

A bike gets its own lift to the top at Sunday River.

4.06 With some condos just in front of you, go left back into the woods.

4.39 You've returned to Lift #2.

You can experience the view from the top of Sunday River, but you're going to have to do some climbing to get there, on:

Sunday Trip 5: Barker Mountain

Distance: *4.22 miles*
Terrain: *Ski-area access roads and trails*
Difficulty: *Moderate*
Time: *45 minutes*
Elevation loss: *1520 feet*
Elevation gain: *520 feet*

0.00 From the top of Lift #6, go left and ride by the Peak Lodge, which is usually closed in summer. At the clearing, go left following the TO FLAT'N 'EM 20 sign.

0.11 *At the T, take the right at the TO BARKER, LOCKE, AND WHITE CAP sign onto the Three Mile Trail (labeled "Last Mile Trail" on Sunday River's map).*

At points this trail was too steep for me to ride.

1.11 *After 20 minutes and 520 feet of gain, you reach the top of the White Cap ski run.*

You can climb the short distance to the actual peak by taking the trail behind the large map of the ski area. This is 2570-foot Barker Mountain. From this peak you can see the highest peak to the north—4180-foot Old Speck Mountain.

Ride back down the same way you came up.

2.12 *At the junction, continue straight on what is Flat'n 'em.*

2.50 *Where Sensation and Flat'n 'em go to the left, veer right and enter the woods on the Moose Tack (Trail) singletrack.*

2.87 *Take the right onto Palisades, another technical singletrack.*

2.95 *Leave the singletrack and go right onto Aurora Peak Road.*

3.32 *A left will take you to the South Ridge trail, but you go straight ahead toward Lift #6. Don't take the lift, but go straight ahead onto #8 Across South Ridge toward the condos. Go left onto the road at the T signed ACROSS SOUTH RIDGE #8/SLALOM COURSE AND TRAINING AREA and descend, then go left onto the trail just before the condos.*

4.22 *You're back at the bottom of Lift #2.*

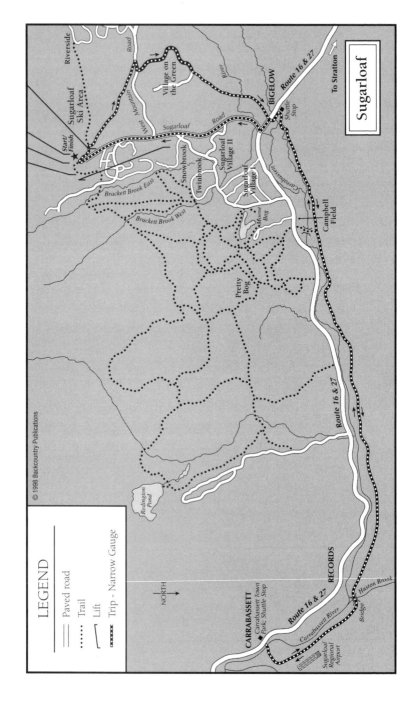

LEGEND

Paved road
.... Trail
— Lift
▪▪▪▪▪ Trip - Narrow Gauge

NORTH →

© 1998 Backcountry Publications

Sugarloaf

Riverside
Road
Village on
the Green
River
BIGELOW
Route 16 & 27
To Stratton
Shuttle
Stop
Shuttle Stop
West Mountain Road
Sugarloaf Ski Area
Sugarloaf Road
Start/Finish
Sugarloaf Village II
Sugarloaf Village I
Snowbrook
Twinbrook
Moose Bog
Carrabassett
Campbell Field
Brackett Brook East
Brackett Brook West
Pretty Bog
Route 16 & 27
Redington Pond
Huston Brook
Bridge
Carrabassett River
Sugarloaf Regional Airport
RECORDS
CARRABASSETT
Carrabassett Town Park; Shuttle Stop
Route 16 & 27

17
Sugarloaf, Maine

Sugarloaf has the reputation of being one of the best, if not *the* best, ski resorts in New England. I've never visited in winter, but I was really looking forward to mountain biking there. What I found, though, was a resort with restaurants, shopping, and a bike shop—but I got the feeling that golf is king (especially when I accidentally wandered out onto the course while attempting to follow a poorly marked trail). If the lift were open and it offered downhill biking, it might be different.Yes, Sugarloaf does have a shuttle bus, and it's a clever attempt to make up for the lack of a lift, but it seems like a long way to go for what it offers. I enjoyed my time there, but I was disappointed.

The Stanley twins, Francis Edgar and Freelan Oscar—named after characters in a Sir Walter Scott novel—were born in Kingfield, Maine, in 1849. By the age of 10, Frank and Freel had built a waterwheel behind their parents' house to conduct mechanical experiments and were running a thriving maple sugar business. Frank was artistic, and began painting using an airbrush of his own patent. He learned to take photographs of his subjects and then airbrush over them. He was dissatisfied with the dry photographic plates of the era, and he and Freel started the Stanley Dry Plate Company in 1883. It was so successful that Eastman Kodak eventually bought them out.

They took the funds from that venture and began the production of steam automobiles. In November 1898, as part of

New England's first car show, an automobile race was held on the ¹/3-mile velodrome in Cambridge, Massachusetts. Francis Stanley drove over to watch the contest and decided, on the spur of the moment, to enter. He ended up winning the race at the breathtaking speed of 27 miles per hour, driving a steamer of his own creation.

In August 1899 Freel and his wife drove one of the Stanley Steamers to the summit of 6288-foot Mount Washington, the highest peak in New England, the first time it had been reached by an automobile. In 1902, the brothers designed and built a new public school for Kingfield, the nearest town to Sugarloaf. It was used until 1980, was saved from demolition, and now serves as the Stanley Museum.

In the Stanleys' day, sugar was sold by the loaf, a cone about 5 inches in diameter. Sugarloaf was named because of the peak's resemblance to a loaf of sugar.

How to get there: From the south, take I-95, the Maine Turnpike, from Portland to Auburn, exit 12, and follow ME 4 north through Farmington. Then pick up ME 27 north and proceed through Kingfield to Sugarloaf.

Total miles of biking available: 53

Season and hours: The Sugarloaf shuttle operates Friday through Sunday, Memorial Day weekend through Columbus Day, 9 AM–4 PM.

Prices: A single ride on the shuttle is $3 ($1 for juniors).

Rental bikes: The Sugarloaf bike shop carries a full line of rental bikes.

Bike shop: Sugarloaf has a full-service pro shop.

Trail identification: Paths are marked by cross-country trail signs and white signs with black arrows.

Special features: Sugarloaf has 53 miles of mountain bike trails on 7000 acres. Instead of using a chairlift, Sugarloaf has a shuttle service. It leaves the main area on the hour and stops at the Riverside cross-country area at 11 minutes after the hour; at Bigelow Station (start of the narrow-gauge railroad bike trail) at 17 minutes after the hour; at the Touring Center at 21 minutes after the hour; and at the Carrabassett town park at 35 minutes past the hour; and loops back to the Touring Center again at 50 minutes after the hour. Sugarloaf hosts a competition clinic on the Friday before the Widowmaker bike race.

Reservation number: 1-800-THE-LOAF

Internet address: http://www.sugarloaf.com/mtnbikehome. html

E-mail address: info@sugarloaf.com

Hiking: Hikes in the Sugarloaf area range from short strolls to ascents of 4237-foot Sugarloaf, 4168-foot Crocker, and 4150-foot Bigelow Peak. Since mountain bikes are essentially absent from the higher-elevation trails, hikers usually have Sugarloaf's upper trails to themselves.

Rider's comment: "Sugarloaf is not my favorite. It's way too far from the nearest highway and not developed enough. The bugs never leave during the summer and it gets too cold in the fall. I would recommend Sunday River over Sugarloaf any day of the week."

Other attractions: Typical summer activities include the Widowmaker Challenge mountain bike race and the Kingfield Festival. Sugarloaf has a golf course, a driving range, tennis and racquetball courts. Every Saturday evening from July 1 to the end of summer, Sugarloaf has a Champagne Moose Express. A 2-day fly-fishing course is held every weekend. Whitewater rafting is offered on the Kennebec and Dead Rivers. Dog-cart rides are offered 0.1 mile north of the Sugarloaf access road on ME 27. The Sugarloaf Sports and Fitness club is a complete gym including massage and hot tubs.

The Kingfield Bank hosts an annual 10K run. The Western Maine Children's Museum (207-235-2211) is open Monday 1–5 PM. Colonel F.B. Morse's 150-year-old wire bridge is just off ME 27, 6 miles south of Kingfield.

Accommodations: Amos G. Winter had the Stanley brothers design and build a mansion for him in Kingfield on the summit of a property known as Winter's Hill. The twins put the boiler from a steam locomotive into the basement and created the first house in Maine with central heat. Amos Jr. taught the kids of Kingfield to ski on the hill and they helped him cut the first ski trails on Sugarloaf Mountain.

Today you can stay in The Inn on Winter's Hill (1-800-233-WNTR), the mansion the Stanleys built for Mr. Winter.

Campground: The Deer Farm campground (207-265-4599) in Kingfield has 47 sites.

Suggested itinerary

Looking for a downhill ride that follows the route of an old railroad and parallels a river with frequent swimming holes? Try:

Sugarloaf Trip 1: Narrow Gauge

Distance: *3.17, 10.90, 16.42, or 18.65 miles*
Terrain: *Ski-area access roads, trails, and paved roads*
Difficulty: *Moderate*
Time: *30 minutes, 1½, 2½, or 3 hours*
Elevation loss: *390 feet*
Elevation gain: *390 to 780 feet*
Special feature: *You can take the shuttle back to Sugarloaf at many points.*

0.00 You start from the bottom of the Super Quad chairlift and go right on a dirt road, unsigned Trail #20, which goes to the left of the maintenance building signed with a black arrow.

168

A professional racer negotiates a grassy singletrack.

1.15 *Turn right onto a dirt road.*

1.26 *Go left onto the dirt road by the large* VILLAGE ON THE GREEN *sign.*

There is also a marker attached to a stop sign, which has the symbol of a bike with the number 26.

2.06 *Turn left at the* VILLAGE GREEN ROAD *sign, which also has a small bike sign.*

2.12 *You turn left onto* FAIRWAY DRIVE, *which narrows to a dirt road.*

2.54 *Where the main dirt road goes left, keep riding straight on a gravel trail that heads toward a pointed peak in the distance.*

This is 4150-foot Bigelow Mountain. You'll come to an unsigned stream crossing. There is not a hint of a trail on the other side of the stream.

Just ride, push, or carry your bike about ⅛ mile through the streambed toward Bigelow.

2.64 *You reach the other side of the convergence of at least two streams and continue riding on the dirt road.*

169

You'll pass the kennels for the Sugarloaf area's dog-cart rides. I had a very nice chat with Tom Diehl, the owner, while his dogs took turns licking me to death.

At the end of the dirt road, cross and go left onto paved ME 16/27.

3.17 *Cross the Carrabassett River and then immediately go right onto a dirt road signed* BIGELOW STATION.

Most railroads were built with 4 feet $8\frac{1}{2}$ inches between the track rails; some, however, were constructed with the rails only 2 or 3 feet apart. These were known as narrow gauge. There was a narrow-gauge railroad, the Kingfield and Dead River, built in 1894 between Kingfield and Bigelow. The old station is still here and is being converted into a private residence. The railroad was such a part of the community that Kingfield has several businesses with the phrase "Narrow Gauge" in their title. This is one of the stops for the Sugarloaf mountain bike shuttle, which stops here at 17 minutes after the hour.

3.37 *Cross a brook on a small wooden bridge and enter the former narrow-gauge railbed, now a recreational trail, signed* WOODABOGAN.

7.42 *You pass an area with beautiful exposed rocks in the Carrabassett River—which make for great swimming holes. Soon you cross an old wooden bridge and then encounter an extremely rocky section. At the T, go right onto a dirt road.*

9.45 *At the end of the dirt road, turn right onto an unsigned paved road.*

9.79 *Just before paved ME 16/27, turn right into the parking lot for the town offices. After 1 ¼ hours you'll reach the Carrabassett town park.*

The Sugarloaf mountain bike shuttle stops here at 35 minutes past the hour. You can return on the shuttle. Or you can return by backtracking.

9.95 *Return to the stop sign, turn left onto the unsigned paved road, and then go left onto dirt Huston Brook Road. Go left onto the narrower trail signed SUGARLOAF and BF.*

You ride across the rough, rocky section, cross the wooden bridge, and then see a sign, which couldn't be seen from the other direction, that says IN MEMORY OF TERRY EGGLETON FOR HIS SUPPORT OF CARRABASSETT VALLEY BIKE PATH.

16.42 *After 2½ hours, you're back at the Bigelow Station.*

Here you can catch the shuttle at 17 minutes after the hour, to avoid the climb back to Sugarloaf, or go left onto paved ME 16/27.

16.65 *After crossing the South Branch of the Carrabassett River, turn right onto the paved Sugarloaf Access Road and begin the tough climb back to the resort.*

18.65 *You're back at the Sugarloaf parking lot.*

Un Canadien Errant

Just a few hours north of the US border are three Canadian resorts that offer mountain bicycling in summer. This is French Canada, and you'll experience the French flavor immediately. Every bridge seems to have pots of flowers to brighten it up, and you'll also notice that all signs are in French—it's against the law of Québec province to have English signs.

The mountain bike trails are no different. RALENTISSEZ tells you to slow down. RETOUR points the way back to the main base. French is also the spoken language. But *"Parlez-vous anglais?"* ("Do you speak English?") opens the door. Even those who answer "Very little" speak well enough to meet most of a cyclist's needs. I don't know if it's because the Tour de France is the most famous bicycle race in the world or because there are so many cycling terms that derive from the French—domestique, derailleur, pannier, peloton, and velodrome—but mountain bicyclists seem very, if not more, welcome north of the border.

And the resorts are different, too. I soon noticed that none of the trails seemed to have water bars. And I knew I was no longer in the United States when I heard a musical advertisement for condoms over a resort's public address system.

In my American chauvinism, I had not expected much from the Canadian resorts. I was therefore shocked when I discovered that one resort was as busy on a weekday as any American resort on a weekend. And I saw protective downhill gear and full-coverage helmets for sale in the shops and being worn on the trails—outside of a race weekend!

Lift tickets here are less expensive than in the United States, and the American dollar is worth more than the Canadian: a double discount.

So start off the morning with a French Canadian breakfast of croissants, fruit, and coffee and enjoy a day on the trails.

Internet address: http://www.infobahnos.com/~swsmith/

18
Bromont, Québec

In 1976, to celebrate the Bicentennial I rode my bike across the United States. One of the unique experiences I had that summer was pulling into a restaurant, campground, or hostel and discovering that almost everyone else there was a fellow cyclist.

There are so many cyclists at Bromont that you can get the same feeling, even on a weekday. This resort, located about halfway between Montréal and Sherbrooke, really caters to the mountain biker. I discovered Bromont on the Internet, where it received glowing reviews.

Stairs accessing the lift have ramps installed at the side, so it's easy to roll bikes up and down. You don't see a building with the word SKI all over it, but instead a building with the phrase SKIS ET VELOS on the side. There's an air hose for filling tires and water hoses for cleaning the bike. It's the only resort I visited whose bike shop carried specialized padded clothing, for the hard-core downhill rider. It's one of two resorts where on a non-race weekend, cyclists were wearing that protective gear. This resort is so popular that on my first trip, on a Tuesday, I knew I was headed in the right direction by the large number of cars with mountain bikes on their racks.

My only complaint at Bromont is that the water park (see "Special features") closes just 20 minutes after the last chairlift to the top.

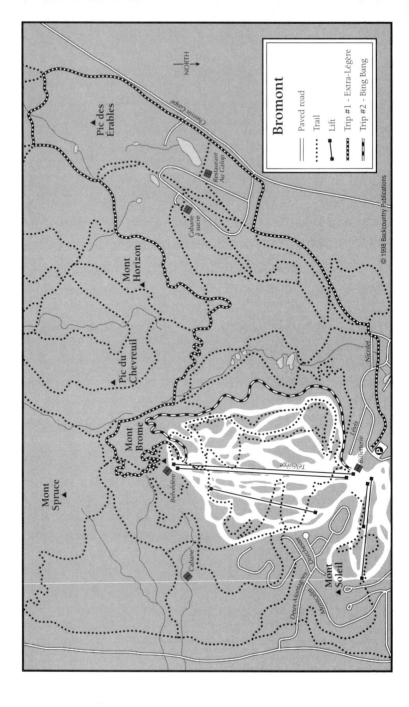

NORTH

Bromont

Paved road
Trail
Lift
Trip #1 - Extra-Légère
Trip #2 - Bing Bang

© 1998 Backcountry Publications

Pic des
Érables

Chemin Gaspé

Restaurant
Au Galop

Cabane
à sucre

Mont
Horizon

Pic du
Chevreuil

Nicolet

Mont
Spruce

Mont
Brome

Belvédère

Lévis

Billetterie

Télésiège

P

Cabane

Dorchester

Monadnocks

Deux-Montagnes

Mont
Soleil

How to get there: From Autoroute 10, take exit 78 and follow
the signs 6 km to Bromont.

Total miles of biking available: 89

The lift: Before taking the lift to the top, you can check the air in
your tires with the hose next to the bike wash, in front of
Sports Experts, a Canadian chain for outdoor enthusiasts.

You reach the 1817-foot (554-meter) summit of Mont
Brome on a double chairlift. People doing the alpine slide
take the same lift, but they get off about halfway up.

Bromont does not use lift tickets; rather, you are issued a
wrist strap, because your admission also includes entry to the
Bromont water park.

The bike hangs by its rear wheel from a hook on the side
of the chair. I prefer this because I can grab a drink of water
from my frame-mounted water bottle on the way up. As you
start the 15-minute ascent to the top you can see, near the
bottom, that one of the trails crosses the alpine slide on a
bridge, and another goes under the slide via a tunnel.

The view from the lift at Bromont is different from that
at any other resort in this book. Unlike most mountains,
which offer views of trees as far as the eye can see, the area
north of Bromont is flat farmland. It resembles Kansas, but
with occasional peaks rising out of the fields.

If you get hungry, there's a restaurant at the base of the lift.

Season and hours: Bromont is open daily from early June to
mid-June and mid-August to late August: 10 AM–4 PM; mid-
June to mid-August: 10 AM–6:30 PM; in September and October, it's open only on weekends, 10 AM–4 PM.

Prices: Prices at Bromont vary according to the time of the year.
A full-day pass is $20.50 ($16 low season) for adults; $15
($13.50 low season) for children 6–11. One ride is $8 for
adults, $6 for children; a family pass is $67. A season pass
costs $75. In late summer they sell passes for half price, or

they'll sell you a season pass for $75, but include in it the following summer.

These prices, in Canadian dollars, are a real bargain, because they include full admission to the water park.

Rental bikes: Bromont has a complete selection of rental bikes both at the on-site Sports Experts (514-534-0357) and at the nearby Chateau Bromont Hotel.

Bike shop: Bromont has a pro bike shop, Sports Experts, at the base.

Trail identification: The trails at Bromont are very well signed, but don't always seem to match the trail map. Nevertheless, you'll have a great time, and will never get lost.

Special features: Bromont has a *lave velo,* or bike wash, where at the end of the day up to a dozen mountain bikers can simultaneously wash their bikes. Most resorts, if they offer a way to clean the bike at all, just provide a hose. At Bromont, you suspend your bike from one of the wheels, so you can even wash the bottom of the frame.

This is a bike-oriented resort whose trail pass includes admission to Bromont Water Park, which has water slides, gravity go-karts, alpine slides, volleyball, the works.

Reservation number: 514-534-2200

Hiking: Hiking is allowed on all trails at Bromont. However, if I were hiking here, because of the number of bikes, I'd stay on the lower-level cross-country trails and surrender the downhill trails to cyclists.

Riders' comments: "At this site, mountain bikers are number one! You aren't treated like a second-class citizen."

"It can be crowded on long weekends and trails get extremely beat up by end of summer."

"Bromont has a good trail map and a good mixture of trails. I tend to ride the longer, more technical singletracks, which are great at Bromont."

Cyclists clean their bikes at the *lave velo* (bike wash) at Bromont.

"There is a good pub called the Golden Lab, which is reasonably priced with good food about 5 minutes from the base by car."

"I highly recommend the Bromont Extra-Légère [#5]. It's not a killer trail, it just rolls, turns, and banks forever at the perfect pitch . . . When ridden fast, it's hard to find a trail that's more enjoyable."

Other activities: Water park, golf, miniature golf, factory outlet stores, a zoo in the nearby town of Granby. The actual village of Bromont, a few kilometers down the hill, exudes French Canadian charm and has shops and restaurants a little more French Canadian than its uphill neighbor.

Festivals: The Coupe du Québec mountain bike race is held here at the end of the summer. Bromont was the site of the equestrian events at the 1976 Montréal Olympics, and every year since then, the city of Bromont has hosted a World Cup Equestrian event.

Campground: Camping Parc Bromont (514-534-2669) has 135 sites and a miniature golf course.

Suggested itinerary

I started off the morning with sweet rolls and decaf coffee at an outdoor café in the village of Bromont, then headed to the resort.

After getting off the lift, you may want to walk or ride the short, steep hill to the right to the *belvédère*, or lookout platform. From there you can see mountains to the south, the trails of the Sutton ski area, and Lac Brome. Now you're ready to tackle some easy to moderate singletracks and trails on Bromont's easiest downhill run:

Bromont Trip 1: Bromont Extra-Légère [Extra Light]

Distance: *6.75 miles (11.25 km)*
Terrain: *Ski-area access roads, trails, and paved roads*
Difficulty: *Moderate*
Time: *1 hour*
Elevation loss: *1394 feet (425 meters)*
Elevation gain: *230 feet (70 meters)*

0.00   You go left following Trail #5, Bromont Extra-Légère.

0.16   After a slight climb, #5 Extra-Légère goes right, then left into the woods of white ash and maple.

This section of the hill is laced with a series of easy switchbacks, but you can detour onto any of several steeper singletracks to make it more difficult. Bromont is the only resort where many of the maple trees are tapped for syrup production.

2.84   #5 Extra-Légère veers to the left on an extremely wide dirt road, then makes an easy-to-miss left turn back onto a trail.

3.91   #5 Extra-Légère goes right onto a dirt road. You climb slightly

and are just above a highway, across the road from a pic-
turesque farm, complete with Holsteins.

5.16   You're now on Trail #1, which crosses a paved road that leads to
an equestrian center and a restaurant.

6.75   After crossing two paved roads, Rue de Charlevoix and Chemin
Champlain, you're back at the parking lot.

You could wear your swimsuit underneath your cycling clothes
and take a dip in the water park between runs, but the day passes
quickly and you may want to wait until the lifts are closed. Have
a snack and then head up the hill again to try some more technical
singletracks:

Bromont Trip 2: Bing Bang
Distance: *3.16 miles (5.26 km)*
Terrain: *Ski-area access roads and trails*
Difficulty: *Moderate*
Time: *50 minutes*
Elevation loss: *1296 feet (395 meters)*
Elevation gain: *131 feet (40 meters)*

0.00   You go left following Trail #5, Bromont Extra-Légère (extra light).

0.09   Go right, then immediately left on #7 Bing Bang, a singletrack.

0.26   After a steep climb, #7 Bing Bang emerges from the woods,
crosses a road, and reenters the trees below an antenna. Imme-
diately go right at the Y in the woods.

2.21   After a big climb, #7 Bing Bang goes right onto Trails #10 and
#12.

2.43   #7 Bing Bang merges to the right with Trail #6.

3.16   You're back at the parking lot.

Bromont has 20 trails to explore. After you've warmed up, you
can work your way up to double black diamonds, such as #18
Adrénaline and #19 Bonzaï.

In theory the lifts close at 4. But that must mean at the top of the lift, because in reality you're not allowed on the lift after 3:40. The water park closes at 4, so this gives you 20 minutes to lock your bike, put on your swimsuit, and go for a dip.

But if you get back after the water park closes, late afternoon is a great time to explore some of the cross-country trails, such as 8.7-mile (14.5 km) #1 Ceinture. The longest and easiest trail at Bromont, it goes around the entire perimeter of the resort.

At the end of the day, you can join other cyclists at the *lave velo*.

19
Mont-Tremblant, Québec

Mont-Tremblant is just what many people are looking for in a resort. Like its American cousin, Stratton, there's a "village" with dining, shopping, and bike shops right at the foot of the hill. You can choose from a variety of restaurants in the village or eat in the lodge on the summit. There is a lake for swimming or boating and a beach for sunning. The extensive network of paved bikeways in and around the village may satisfy many visitors' desire for a bike ride. Condos are at the base of the mountain; campgrounds are nearby. The only drawback at Mont-Tremblant is that there are really only $2\frac{1}{2}$ (one trail has two options at midmountain) ways down that are available to mountain cyclists.

The Native Americans in the Tremblant region felt that if the purity of the mountains was ever disturbed, Manitou, the God of the Wilderness, would make the mountains tremble.

In 1858 William Logan, a geologist, said that the Natives called Tremblant Manitonga Soutana or the Mountain of the Devil because they heard or felt the earth trembling. It is believed that because of the rumbling noises produced by the streams as they roared down the mountain, the settlers changed Manitonga Soutana to Montagne Tremblante ("trembling mountain") and named the river that flows down from Tremblant Devils' River.

Parc Mont-Tremblant, the largest and oldest of Québec's 17 provincial parks, was created in 1859. By 1869, nearby St.-Jovite had been settled.

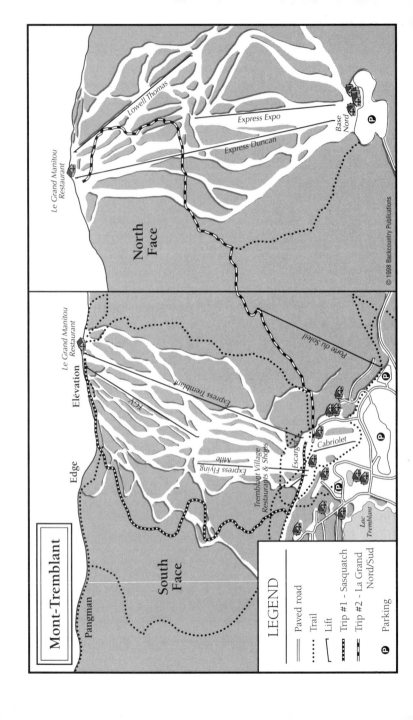

Mont-Tremblant

North Face

South Face

Le Grand Manitou Restaurant

Lowell Thomas

Express Expo

Express Duncan

Base Nord

Elévation

Edge

TGV

Express Tremblant

Express Flying Mile

Porte du Soleil

Pangman

Tremblant Village Restaurants & Shops

Escarg

Cabriolet

Lac Tremblant

© 1998 Backcountry Publications

LEGEND

Paved road
Trail
Lift
Trip #1 - Sasquatch
Trip #2 - La Grand Nord/Sud
Parking

Jackrabbit Johannsen, a Norwegian, escorted the first skiers onto Mont-Tremblant. In 1932—even though Tremblant lacked trails or lifts—he convinced the Canadian Amateur Ski Association to hold its first Kandahar race. By 1939 a chairlift was taking skiers to the summit and the Mont-Tremblant Lodge opened.

How to get there: Mont-Tremblant is located on Highway 322, 75 miles (120 km) north of Montréal via Autoroute 15 and Highway 117.

Total miles of biking available: 28

The lift: The main lift at Tremblant is the Tremblant Express, a four-person detachable quad with a Plexiglas canopy that protects riders in cold weather. The lift attendants even hand out blankets (to everyone but the hardy mountain cyclists) on cool summer mornings. On the 17-minute journey to the top you pass, between pine trees, over a stream spanned by a wooden footbridge.

On the summit is Le Grand Manitou lodge, which has a restaurant, gift shop, rest rooms, a water fountain, and a pay phone. The deck of the lodge offers a panoramic view of the Tremblant area including the region's two lakes, Lac Tremblant and Lac Oimet. The summit also has numerous chairs from which to enjoy the view. An information booth in front of the lodge has pictures, labeled in French, identifying many of the native trees. On the other side of the summit is the hiking center, which has a great view into the Tremblant wilderness from the back deck.

A *douche à velo,* or "bike wash," is located between Le Cabriolet and the Tremblant Express.

Season and hours: The lift is open 10 AM–5 PM (on weekends till 9 PM) from late June to mid-October.

Prices: An all-day pass is $15 ($12 for juniors). A single trip costs $12 ($10 for juniors). A family day pass (good for two

Cyclists fly through the wooded trails of Mont-Tremblant, Québec.

adults and four children) is $35. A season pass is $60 ($48 for juniors). All prices are Canadian.

Rental bikes: Rental bikes are available in the village at Magasin de la Place (819-681-3000, ext. 4502) and at Chalet des Voyageurs (819-681-3000, ext. 5579).

Bike shop: The above shops also offer repairs and accessories.

Trail identification: Trails are well marked with brown wooden signs. Even on singletracks where there are no options, the trees have been blazed with orange arrows.

Special features: The village at Mont-Tremblant is a re-creation of old Québec City, with almost as many shops and cafés as the original. You and your bike reach the village from the parking lot on Le Cabriolet, a six-person, detachable, stand-up "platform." You just walk your bike on, and ride the free lift to the village. At lunch or at the end of the day, restaurants in the village offer a variety of cuisines from around the world, including French, Thai, and Mexican.

Reservation numbers: 819-681-3000, ext. 6642, or 1-800-461-8711

Internet address: http://www.cam.org/~sailor/chair.htm

Hiking: Mont-Tremblant offers 23 km of hiking trails. One trip up the lift is $10 ($6 for juniors).

Rider's comment: "Mont-Tremblant Park is a *fantastic* place to ride. The park is huge and there are trails just about everywhere. It's also a great place to take a multiday biking/camping trip."

Other activities: There are 19 km of paved bike trails at the base of the mountain, connecting all parts of the resort. Just off Route 117, on Route 322, you pass the Parc Lineaire, a 200 km bike path that runs from St. Jerome north to Mont-Laurier. Other activities include golf, tennis, beach, sailing, in-line skating, and the Tremblant Kidz Club. Tremblant Academy (1-800-461-8711) offers seminars in personal and business development. And the Boutique Expedition (819-681-4646) offers courses in rock climbing, canoeing, kayaking, hiking, and orienteering. The Centre Nautique on Lac Tremblant offers water skiing, windsurfing, and pontoon boats. If downhill mountain biking isn't fast enough for you, the Jim Russell Racing School (819-425-2739) offers classes in automobile racing on the 4.4 km Le Circuit Mont-Tremblant. And just like Québec City, Tremblant offers horse-drawn carriage rides around the village.

Festivals: Activities during a typical summer might include St.-Jean Baptiste Celebrations, Canada Day, the 24 Hours of Adrenaline (a mountain bike race), Family Festival, Canadian 5K Open Water Swimming Championship, Tremblant Blues Festival, and the Octoberfest.

Campgrounds: Camping de la Diable (819-425-5501) has 178 sites. Camping Laurien (514-467-2518) has 330 sites.

Hostel: At the Domaine du Beau Sejour (1110 Chemin Saindon,

Labelle, Québec JOT 1H0; 819-686-1323), 25 minutes north of Mont-Tremblant, you can swim from the hostel's private beach.

Suggested itinerary

For vacationers looking for a flat, paved ride, Tremblant's 11.8 miles (19 km) of bike paths may be ideal. But the downhill enthusiast will probably want to start out on a moderate run that offers a combination of roads and singletracks with great views of the Parc Tremblant wilderness and Lac Tremblant:

Mont-Tremblant Trip 1: La Sasquatch
Distance: *3.81 miles (6.13 km)*
Terrain: *Ski-area access roads and trails*
Difficulty: *Moderate*
Time: *50 minutes*
Elevation loss: *2080 feet (635 meters)*
Elevation gain: *50 feet (15 meters)*

0.00 *After getting off the lift, go left following La Sasquatch trail, a wide, rocky gravel road.*

You soon arrive at an overlook with a sign that identifies the peaks left to right as: les Trois Soeurs (the three sisters), Pic Pangman, Pic Johannsen, Pic Edge, Montagne du Perches, la Vache Noire (the black cow), Mont Carcan, and Mont Nixon. The footpath to the left, by another information sign, leads to the summit of a small peak.

Continuing on the trail, you descend and have a magnificent view of Lac Tremblant to your left.

0.40 *Leave the gravel road and go right on Sasquatch Trail, a moderately difficult singletrack.*

0.69 *You leave the singletrack and go left onto another dirt road.*

© HENRY GEORGI/MONT-TREMBLANT

Baptism of mud at Mont-Tremblant

0.75   Leave the road and go right onto a singletrack that climbs to give you another view of Lac Tremblant. You'll ride through a damp area with moss and ferns, and cross a small bridge just before the singletrack ends.

1.92   After descending 1035 feet (315 meters) in 30 minutes, you cross a dirt road and reenter the woods on the singletrack. Then you go right on a dirt road and enter la forêt enchantée, "the enchanted forest."

The last two sections of singletrack have NORBA vertical arrows but they aren't as hard as the previous sections. Now you exit the woods but are not allowed to descend on the gravel road. Instead you're restricted to a path on the left side of the road, which turns to the left and leads you back into the woods. You cross a wooden bridge and then encounter a very rough ride over poles that have been laid across a muddy section.

You leave the singletrack and go left onto a dirt road by a BASE SUD 500 M *sign.*

3.81   When you pass a dam with a waterfall, you're back at the base.

After a snack at one of Tremblant Village's many cafés or on the deck of the summit lodge, you're ready for a longer trail with more climbing:

Mont-Tremblant Trip 2: La Grand Nord/La Nord-Sud
Distance: *5.70 miles (9.18 km)*
Terrain: *Ski-area access roads and trails*
Difficulty: *Moderate*
Time: *1 hour*
Elevation loss: *2360 feet (720 meters)*
Elevation gain: *395 feet (120 meters)*

0.00   After leaving the lift, you cross the summit and head to the right of the Hiking Centre. Then you enter La Grand Nord trail, a sin-

gletrack that winds through a pine forest.

2.42   At the T, go right following the LA NORD-SUD TO BASE SUD 6.5 KM *sign.*

You may encounter uphill traffic on this two-way trail, which passes through a really nice section of exposed rock.

3.83   At the junction with La Chouette, go straight on Nord-Sud.

You cross two streams on log bridges and ride over many water bars that are spanned by small log bridges.

5.04   Crest a hill and you'll come to two spots from which you have excellent views of Lac Tremblant and the new Tremblant Village.

5.70   You're back at the bottom of the hill.

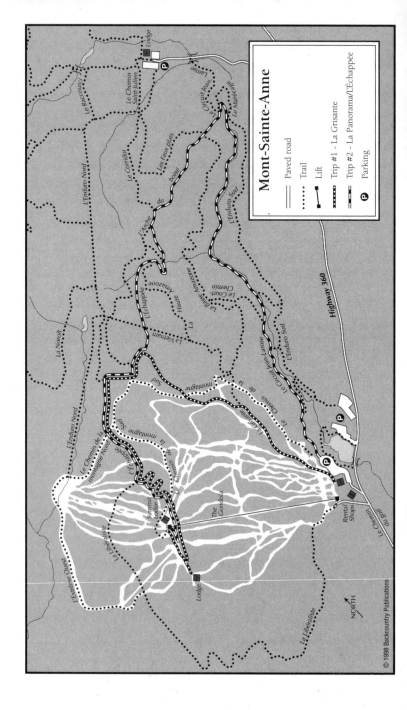

Mont-Sainte-Anne

— Paved road
.... Trail
▬■▬ Lift
▬▬ Trip #1 - La Grisante
▬▬ Trip #2 - La Panorama/L'Échappée
Ⓟ Parking

Highway 360

Lodge

Le Raccourci

Le Chemin Saint-Julien

L'Enduro Nord

Le Corridor

Les Faux plats

L'Arche du bois

L'Échappée

La Noroît

L'Enduro Nord

Chemin de la montagne Nord

L'Extrême Ouest

La Libéraline

Chemin de la montagne Sud

Summit Lodge

Le Chemin de la montagne

Le Chemin de la montagne Sud

The Gondola

Lodge

La Libéraline

NORTH

Circuit Jean Larose

Le Marécage

Circuit Jean Larose

L'Enduro Sud

Le Court-Chemin

La Haute Amazone

La Basse Amazone

Le Viêtnam

Le Chemin Jean Larose

L'Enduro Sud

Rental Shops

Le Chemin du golf

© 1998 Backcountry Publications

20
Mont-Sainte-Anne, Québec

Mont-Sainte-Anne really has it all. It has perhaps one of the most extensive networks of trails open to mountain bikers. You can stay at a condo at the base of the mountain or ride to the mountain along a bikeway from a nearby campground. It has superb views of the St. Lawrence River and of the undeveloped wilderness to the north. Routes range from easy cross-country trails at the base (essentially bikeways) to the brutal Vietnam downhill. And you're close to the shopping, dining, and accommodations of Québec City.

People began skiing on Mont-Sainte-Anne in 1944, and the Canadian Downhill Championships were held there in 1947. There was no lift, though, and the ascent took about 3 hours, but hardy souls continued to ski there. The current resort opened in 1966, with 10 trails, four lifts, and the only gondola in eastern Canada. With the opening up of 90 km of cross-country trails, the Junior World Nordic Championships were held here in 1972. By the end of the 1970s, there were 14 lifts and the gondola served 27 trails. Today Mont-Sainte-Anne offers the mountain bicyclist 200 km of downhill and cross-country trails to explore. Mont-Sainte-Anne is so popular with cyclists that six Mountain Bike World Cup competitions have been held here since 1991, attracting 2000 competitors from 35 countries.

If you judge your mountain biking experience by the amount of mud you and your bike pick up, then you'll love Mont-Sainte-Anne! Some of the trails here are so muddy that not only are there places to wash the bikes, but the resort also provides showers for the cyclists. This is the muddiest I've been since playing football on a rain-soaked field in high school.

How to get there: From Québec, take Autoroute 40, which becomes Highway 138. In Québec City, take Highway 440 east for 10 km (6 miles). This road becomes Highway 138 east, where you go for 25 km (15 miles) until you reach Highway 360. Take this road 3 km to the access to the Parc Mont-Sainte-Anne.

Total miles of biking available: 86

The lift: You ride to the 800-meter summit inside an eight-passenger gondola, la télécabine. From the parking lot I kept waiting for the lift to open. I finally realized I was looking at a chairlift with a plastic bubble and not the gondola, which is not visible from the parking lot.

Like Cranmore (see chapter 12), the lift ticket is attached to an elastic cord. You either hang it around your neck or attach it to your bike. To enter the lower gondola station, you need to insert your lift ticket into a slot on a turnstile.

Unlike any other resort, you load your own bike onto the exterior racks. The gondola can carry two bikes on the front and two bikes on the back.

During the 13½-minute ride to the summit, you ascend between stands of maple trees and have fantastic views of the resort, the St. Lawrence River, and the Île d'Orléans.

The upper gondola station, which has a drinking fountain, seems to act as a funnel for cool air. It was quite chilly inside the station, but as soon as I got out onto the trail I was comfortable.

Season and hours: Mid-June to mid-October, 10 AM–5 PM.

Prices: Full day $18; single trip $12 ($10 juniors). A trail pass is $5; a season pass costs $125.

Rental bikes: Sports Experts rents full-suspension bikes for $50 per day, or $20 per hour. Regular bikes are $33 per day, or $12 per hour. If you rent a bike, you get a 50 percent discount on the gondola.

Bike shop: Mont-Sainte-Anne has two bike shops at the resort. In addition, 1 km below the resort is Bicycles Marius (418-827-2420).

Trail identification: Mont-Sainte-Anne is well marked with permanent steel signs.

Special features: At the northeast corner of the parking lot is a course for observed trials competition. Mont-Sainte-Anne offers a day camp for children 4–14 years of age. For groups, the resort can arrange for multiday outings. You spend the nights in a shelter and your luggage can be transported in a shuttle.

Reservation number: 1-800-463-1568 allows you to book a room in one of more than 45 lodging establishments in the area.

Internet address: http://plato.gmt.ulaval.ca/voronoi/beland/mont.htm

Hiking: Mont-Sainte-Anne has over 20 km of hiking trails. The Merrell Hiking Centre offers maps and rents hiking boots.

Riders' comments: "First of all, Mont-Sainte-Anne is huge! I usually try to stay away from biking areas that are situated on super-large ski hills . . . but the area is so big that there is an abundance of flatter singletracks . . . The mountain usually holds at least one mega race each year. The big race weekends are a real blast! A lot of the riders consider this stop on their race schedule to be the premier party spot, and lot of the big riders are at the party."

"If you have a problem with your bike, you don't have to go into town to find a shop."

"At night you can go into Québec City and eat at a great restaurant."

Trail signs measure distances in kilometers at Mont-Sainte-Anne.

"The back side has a great backcountry feel to it, as you almost never see anything man-made. On hot days, you'll want to stop for a quick dip in the river, close to Chalet Marie-Josée."

Other attractions: Tourist attractions include the world-famous Catholic shrine at nearby Sainte-Anne-de-Beaupré; Cap Tourmante is a National Bird Sanctuary; scenic "chutes" or waterfalls include the Canyon des Chutes Sainte-Anne, the Sept-Chutes, and the Chute Montmorency. The Île d'Orléans is only minutes away.

Mont-Sainte-Anne is about 30 minutes north of Québec City, one of only two walled cities in North America. After a day of mountain biking, you can enjoy the cuisine of one of Québec's many restaurants.

Mont-Sainte-Anne has two 18-hole golf courses. In-line skates (*patins en ligne*) can be rented and used on over 3 km of trails, including a speed oval. The resort also offers paragliding. Both tandem flights and lessons are available, starting at $70.

Festivals: Expo-Québec (an agricultural fair) is held in late August; Mont-Sainte-Anne holds an autumn festival; and on Sundays through Thanksgiving weekend (mid-October in Canada) there is a musical brunch.

Campground: Mont-Sainte-Anne has a campground with 166 sites just a few km uphill from the resort. Easy cross-country trails connect it to the base of the mountain. The campground offers swimming, complete with a beach, water slides, and fishing. There's also a petting zoo, an indoor game room, a playground, movies, and giant checker and chess games.

Hostel: The Centre International de Séjour de Québec (19 rue Ste.-Ursule, Québec; 418-694-0755) is in the heart of Old Québec, about 30 minutes from Mont-Sainte-Anne.

Suggested Itinerary

Mont-Sainte-Anne's shortest trail, a mixture of trails and moderate singletracks, with views of the St. Lawrence and Île d'Orléans, would be a long route anywhere else:

Sainte-Anne Trip 1: La Grisante

Distance: *5.23 miles (2.85 km)*
Terrain: *Ski-area access roads and trails*
Difficulty: *Moderate*
Time: *50 minutes*
Elevation loss: *2100 feet (640 meters)*
Elevation gain: *15 feet (5 meters)*

0.00 Leave the upper gondola station and immediately go left following the trail signed L'ÉCHAPPÉE 18 KM/LA GRISANTE 9 KM.

You descend on a wide, almost flat, gradual dirt downhill.

0.49 *After an easy, almost flat descent with little jumps, you arrive at the Chalet de la Crête lodge.*

The views from the multilevel decks on the south side are stunning. You are looking back into several hundred years of French Canadian history as you see the St. Lawrence, used by explorers, settlers, soldiers, and traders, the Île d'Orléans, and Québec City in the distance to the west. To the north is pure wilderness, unsettled and pristine for several thousand years.

You take the road back toward the lifts.

0.69 *Go right at the* LA GRISANTE *8.4 KM/*L'ÉCHAPPÉE *17.4 KM sign onto a singletrack.*

1.46 *There is the first of many stop signs, which you encounter before crossing a dirt road.*

1.87 *At the junction where La Liberaliste goes left, go right on L'Échappée and La Grisante.*

2.87 *At a T, La Grisante and L'Échappée go right on a trail signed* L'ARCHE DU BOISÉ.

3.19 *La Grisante and L'Échappée go right, leaving L'Arche du boisé.*

3.27 *At the junction of La Grisante and L'Échappée, go right on La Grisante.*

3.76 *At a stop sign, you leave the singletrack and La Grisante becomes an uphill gravel road straight ahead, which soon becomes a wide, rocky area with a partial view of the Île d'Orléans.*

5.23 *You're back at the base area.*

Now you're ready for a mixture of trails and singletracks that ends up on a rolling dirt road:

Sainte-Anne Trip 2: La Panorama/L'Échappée

Distance: *9.80 miles (15.78 km)*
Terrain: *Ski-area access roads and trails*

Difficulty: *Moderate*
Time: *1 1/2 hours*
Elevation loss: *2085 feet (635 meters)*
Elevation gain: *115 feet (35 meters)*

0.00 Leave the upper gondola station and immediately go left following the trail signed L'ÉCHAPPÉE 18 KM/LA GRISANTE 9 KM. You descend on a wide, almost flat, gradual dirt downhill.

0.34 Go left on La Grisante/L'Échappée.

2.51 At a T, La Grisante and L'Échappée go right on a trail signed L'ARCHE DU BOISÉ.

2.91 Go left onto L'Échappée (the escape).

3.12 Cross the Vietnam Trail, and after getting through a muddy, rocky section of trail, go left onto La Haute Amazone (the high Amazon).

4.27 Where Amazone goes left, you go to the right on L'Échappée and then cross a stream on a twisted wooden bridge.

4.69 L'Échappée merges with L'Arche du boisé (bridge of trees) and then goes right.

5.54 You go left on Les Faux plats (the false plates).

5.85 L'Échappée goes right on a gravel road and joins Le Circuit Jean-Larose, an easy, rolling route.

9.45 You reach the parking lot. At the northeastern corner is an observed trials bike course.

Let Backcountry Guides Take You There

More Biking Guides

In New England and the Northeast

25 Bicycle Tours in Maine
25 Mountain Bike Tours in Massachusetts
25 Bicycle Tours on Cape Cod and the Islands
25 Mountain Bike Tours in Vermont
25 Bicycle Tours in Vermont
30 Bicycle Tours in the Finger Lakes Region
25 Mountain Bike Tours in the Hudson Valley
25 Bicycle Tours in the Hudson Valley
25 Bicycle Tours in the Adirondacks

In the Mid-Atlantic States

25 Bicycle Tours in Maryland
25 Bicycle Tours on Delmarva
25 Bicycle Tours in Eastern Pennsylvania
30 Bicycle Tours in New Jersey
25 Mountain Bike Tours in New Jersey
25 Bicycle Tours in and around Washington, D.C.

Farther South, Farther West

25 Bicycle Tours in Ohio's Western Reserve
25 Bicycle Tours in Southern Indiana
30 Bicycle Tours in Wisconsin
25 Bicycle Tours in the Twin Cities and Southeastern Minnesota
25 Bicycle Tours in Coastal Georgia and the Carolina Low Country
25 Bicycle Tours in the Texas Hill Country and West Texas

We offer many more books on hiking, fly fishing, travel, nature, and other subjects. Our books are available at bookstores and outdoor stores everywhere. For more information or a free catalog, please call 1-800-245-4151 or write to us at The Countryman Press, PO Box 748, Woodstock, Vermont 05091. You can find us on the Internet at www.countrymanpress.com.